NORTH & SOUTH

to hell with

to hell with

JOURNALS Edition A: NORTH & SOUTH

PUBLISHED BY TO HELL WITH PUBLISHING
LAURENCE JOHNS & DEAN RICKETTS

EDITED BY LEE BRACKSTONE

EDITORIAL:
LAURENCE JOHNS, KEVIN CONROY SCOTT,
LISA BAKER, LUCY OWEN, HELEN FRANCIS

CONSULTANTS:
MIGUEL AGUILAR, LOUISE BEHRE, HANIF KUREISHI,
ANDREW O'HAGAN, DBC PIERRE, DEBORAH ROGERS

CONTENTS

JOHN BURNSIDE

IDEAS OF NORTH

I   70° N

In dreams, there are two possible selves. One is the named, delimited, social being: the self we refer to when we speak of personality, or character, (and the object to which Paul of Tarsus refers when he says, "God is no respecter of persons"). The other is at once more elusive and more sharply defined, a creature we could talk about - mistakenly, I think - as the true, or the inner; the self who inhabits the poem by Emily Dickinson:

> I dwell in Possibility -
> A fairer House than Prose -
> More numerous of Windows -
> Superior - for Doors -
>
> Of Chambers as the Cedars -
> Impregnable of Eye -
> And for an Everlasting Roof
> The Gambrels of the Sky -
>
> Of Visitors - the fairest -
> For Occupation – This -
> The spreading wide my narrow Hands
> To gather Paradise -

To call this self 'inner' is a mistake, I think, because it is anything but inward. Every religious and philosophical tradition that speaks of the soul locates it, for the most part, as far from the everyday self as anything can be, a creature of wider or subtler places than the spaces we can occupy. To call it 'the true self' is also a mistake because, much as we would like to imagine otherwise, the public - the conventional, the logical, the social, the waking - is just as true, (if true means anything at all in this case) and just as capable of becoming authentic, as the private and the spiritual. Still, in a society that is bound to overvalue the perceptible and, in all manner of hidden and subtle ways, the tractable self, that remote and autonomous creature who

never sets foot in the visible world - the secret being, the non-person
that we sometimes refer to as soul or spirit - is more precious to the
imagination and more worthy of pursuit than the self who fills the tax
return, or mops up after the baby. When we dream, we sometimes
become visitors in that soul's domain: there is a house, a garden, a
landscape, a middle distance, a sky in that place which cannot be
found elsewhere, and each of these is an aspect of the soul or spirit self
that belongs, not to me, or to the world, but somewhere else, somewhere
that cannot be *occupied*. For each of us, that landscape is different, just
as each of us has different gods, or different notions of god's absence;
for me, it is a line I have only crossed four or five times in my life, a
line that runs across the top of the world, just missing Murmansk and
the Bering Strait, an imaginary line, invented by mapmakers, but no
less real for that.

Above this line, maps tend to make everything white, just as they
once left the African interior blank, or annotated with dire warnings
about monsters – and in both cases, the error has much to do with a
local blindness: the inability, say, of European cartographers to imagine
an unknown continent as anything other than a habitat for the
uncivilised, or the inability of the uneducated eye, confronting the
farthest north, to see beyond the forms and textures with which it is
familiar. The African interior was empty because no civilised man
cared to imagine it as much like his own world, with networks of
family and tribe and commerce, where people much like himself
engaged in the beautiful commonplaces of domestic life and the
delicious complexities of art, or legislation. The northern wilderness
is white because our eyes are not quite up to the long gaze, our ears
have not learned how to listen to its wide expanses, our minds are
unequipped for the fine details of texture and light that make up this
seemingly featureless land. The real land - the real interior, the real
north - is mostly invisible to us because, all too often, we are too
limited in vision and too ungenerous of imagination to see it. Politically,
the consequences of this blindness have been a series of tedious and
painfully familiar narratives of failure and barbarity, 'frontier' stories
of invasion and expropriation, from the 'Norwegianisation' of the
Sàmi, to the Manifest Destiny of the American west, to the current
occupation of Palestine.

Spiritually, however, the idea of north, (like the idea of wilderness, or the interior), is a wholly different matter, a notion that, if anything, stands in opposition to the savagery of the frontiersman. Spiritually, the concern is with whiteness and with the implied preservation of the holy ground - a ground that cannot be occupied, only passed through, only briefly and tentatively *inhabited*. Because, in truth, it is not the 'real' land but the white space on the map that the spirit inhabits. The white space of the far north or the unknown interior; the sound of a place name; the invisible territory that lies between one page of an atlas and another. It is not the land itself; it is not place. Always and everywhere, somebody else lives there. Always and everywhere, no matter how empty it might seem, the world is peopled, and so occupied, and the country to which the soul belongs is the very antithesis of occupation.

II   White Nights

Sometimes I dream of the last bed, the one I will die in. It is white of course – in dreams all beds are white – and mercifully narrow, because I hope to die alone, after making the necessary farewells. People say, with regret, that we all die alone, but who would wish it otherwise? Who would wish to be accompanied into that terminal whiteness? The necessary farewell means nothing, unless it contains the wish that the other may continue living, for as long as possible, in this good world - a wish that is usually unspoken, but always understood.

The white of the bed in my dream, and in the perfect death, is the same white that one finds on maps of the far north. The same white that we carry with us when we carry an idea of north. Not just the pure, cold white of permafrost, but also the white of summer nights in Alta, or Lakselv, a white that is neither pure nor cold, but full of suggestion, hazy with the possibility of new arrivals and fresh departures, 'of Chambers as the Cedars', a bourn to which all things come, in order to be transformed, and so to begin once more.

III   70° N

Some years ago, I was introduced to Hans-Ragnar Mathisen, the Sámi artist and activist. I had brought along a copy of his Sámi Atlas, in which, (among many other wonderful and fascinating things), he presents a view of the Earth as seen from the top, with the North Pole at its centre, the land we think of as the remote north, including Sápmi, the Sàmi homeland, near the middle and everything else tailing away, with Chicago and Moscow near the very edges of the map, and countries we think of as important or at least vast, dwarfed by the polar icefields and Greenland, (the book contains another view, from the South Pole, in which the immensity of Antarctica is fully registered, compensating finally for all those globes and charts in which the far north - and the far south - dwindled to almost nothing. The Sámi Atlas also contains details of Sámi geography, history and culture that have been ignored for centuries by a world that, for the most part, saw Sámi people as peripheral to the political, social and cultural realities, just as they saw their homeland as a mere source of 'resources'.

An admirer of Mathisen's work, I had brought the Atlas to be signed. Later, when I opened the book and read the inscription, I was taken aback. It said, simply:

See, and learn!

Of course, I understood the meaning of these words and, in the context, their directness was entirely appropriate. I had come to Mathisen's home as a serious researcher, making a radio programme about the Sámi circumpolar festival, Riddu Riddu, and I wanted some background: stories, for example, about the difficult and painful era of the Alta Dam protest, when the Sámi took on the might of the Oslo government and, even while losing the river, (one the most beautiful rivers in the world, and a source of livelihood and spiritual nourishment to many), won something of a moral victory, one that led to the creation of a Sámi parliament at Kárasjohka, and an increased awareness of Sámi culture and politics. Stories about his childhood, when he was taken from his family and given a Norwegian education, or about recent developments in the 'exploitation of natural resources' on the *Finnmarksvidda*, (a process akin to the proposed development of the 'Alaskan Wilderness', in which oil and power companies were scouting the *vidda*, a place of immense natural beauty, vital to the reindeer-herding way of life, for untapped carbon fuel deposits). At the end of our discussion, when I was about to leave, Hans Ragnar said, quietly, but with real force, "Tell them what is happening. Tell them what the Oslo government is doing to us!". For me, it was a deeply disturbing moment: Oslo was synonymous with peacemaking, especially in the Middle East and Norway, in spite of recent political changes, had always been (and still is) seen as enlightened and just the very model of a civil society. Not long before our meeting, I had seen people on the farthest north protesting on National Day by waving hundreds of plain, white flags in place of the usual Norwegian banners, flags that were meant to remind their countrymen in the south - politely, and with excruciating humility - not to forget them or their increasingly damaged land. It was a reminder that cut me - an outsider, a tourist, really - to the quick: as one for whom the north has always been the locus of dreams and imaginings, I need it to remain undamaged, true to itself, a fit place for those who belong there to dwell in. To keep that clear, white space on the map where the concerns of the south dwindle away, I need the northlands to continue *as north*, not as a playground or fuel store for the south. To inhabit my own land fully, I need the Arctic charr and the Arctic poppy, the polar bear and the reindeer, the Sámi and the Fenns, to go on living as they have always lived, not in some static world of children's picture books and National Geographic features, but moving through space and time as they choose to do, according to their natures. Without them, there can be no idea of north, even here, in the rooms of my imagination. Without yielding up the far north to the just possession of those who belong there, I will never find it when I need it, never be able to puzzle over, and find nourishment in, its myths and songs and strange weather. Without the north, the south is nowhere, and a world that navigates by an atlas in which the details of the Sámesiiddat have been omitted is a world impoverished beyond belief, a world that might just as well cease to exist.

IV   The Last Glacier

Ten thousand years ago the last glacier melted in Fife.
Melting ice water formed Loch Leven and flowed down
the river Leven.

But people have now dammed and regulated the loch,
which was once much larger.

From a display in the Kirkcaldy Art Museum

Sometimes, watching a documentary about dinosaurs, or the coming
ecological disaster, I remember that I am haunted by glaciers. It is a
purely physical affair, this haunting: my skin is a net of desires, but the
strongest of these is the desire for some prehistoric chill and the
deepest thirst I know is the thirst for ancient, unpolluted water from
the core of the permafrost. What bothers me most about the ubiquitous
narratives of ecological disaster and degradation is not the idea that
the earth will be destroyed, (it will not, because it has seen all of this
before), or that, in spite of everything we know and fear, nobody is doing
anything about it; what bothers me is the simple fact that the ice cap
is melting. On a museum exhibit, the fact that a great glacier, the last
of many, disappeared into a loch a few miles from my house may be
nothing more than a matter of curiosity; the damming and regulation
and the diminishment of the loch, however, remind me of our one last
universal tragedy. Soon, what we think of, when we think of ice, will be
something other than it is now: like the glacier, our idea of a permanent,
ordered, nourishing cold will eventually decay, to be replaced by
something anecdotal and inconsequential, like the gobbets of ice in a
fridge freezer. For the sake of a certain, very specific diversity - a
diversity, not just of Arctic flora and fauna, but of the imagination itself
- we need the glaciers and the icecaps. To lose the polar bear or the
Arctic poppy would be one form of tragedy; to lose that recess of the
mind where we conceive the idea of north would be another. Some might
say that dreams and ideas are less important than flesh and leaf;
surely, by now, it is obvious that the two go together and that neither
can prosper without the other.

V   70° N

A few autumns ago, I borrowed a car and drove north from Tromsø to Alta. It was a magical journey. I was alone on the road, for the most part; the tourist season - when convoys of camper vans and mobile homes from Europe head for the Nordkapp to buy "I have seen the Midnight Sun" stickers, spewing out great piles of banana skins and tin cans and cigarette stubs as they go – the 'season' which is no season at all was over and, though the weather was still fair, the hotels and campsites were closed. I was driving alone, stopping from time to time at little settlements along the coast: a tourist, nothing more. I had no camera, no maps, nothing I was intent on seeing, but I had a tourist's eye for the racks of fish drying on the shore, and a tourist's sense of the land as strange and wonderful, rolling the place-names around on my tongue, jotting down details and reminders, the jottings of a tourist, surprised to find echoes in the landscape of paintings I had seen in the National Art Museum in Oslo, or the books I had read at home, dreaming my idea of north. Sometimes I think that's all there is to any kind of journey: to be a tourist who doesn't like tourists. To have that tourist's mentality - a beginner's mentality - without wanting to go anywhere that a tourist might go.

Eventually, I fetched up in a borrowed house on the edge of Alta. Nobody else was about, but food and drink had been left for me and a bed had been made up, because people who choose to live in the north are generous more often than not and, tired after the drive, I had a quick supper and retired. My bed was on the north side of the house, perched in an angle of wind and it was the wind that both kept me awake for hours and fed me - the way music, or touch feeds us - all through the night, through waking and sleep, and through absence and dreams: a long, inventive variation on a theme I had been presumptuous enough to imagine I knew inside out. At home, I think of the wind the way one might think of a friendly animal, as it comes to touch me then flickers away, a running question, a recurring memory of *wild*. Here, though, it came off the sea and fingered the walls, it wrapped itself around the flagpole just outside my window, intimate, searching, as if it were searching for something it remembered from long ago, the way the old Sámi wind god, Bieggaålmaj, remembers the land and, with a fleeting touch, calls it into being. The difference, in that small room at the top of Europe, was that Bieggaålmaj remembered - was, moment by moment, remembering - *me*. Weeks later, when I got home, the wind touched me again, and it was different. A southern wind, moving from one form to another like a lost spirit: not a man, or a woman, not even a child, but the animal spirit that passes through everyone – man, woman, child – a spirit that takes up residence for a time before moving on, following the path it knows, the path of itself, a path that leads everywhere. There was something beautiful about this wind, even if was lost but, for me, Bieggaålmaj was gone. This wind remembered the land I occupied in snatches and glimpses, but it made no sense of the whole, it bound nothing together, and it did not remember me, as a soul, or as a person. In this wind, I did not exist – and I was glad of the fact.

VI   Bieggaålmaj

In dreams there are two selves. Both are true, both are real, but the wind god only remembers one of them. When I dream of the last version of myself - my last body, the one I will die in - I dream of something white and spare, a body that can cling to nothing, a body that will pull nothing down with it. Bieggaålmaj blows through this body, just as he blows through the last bed, and the furthest whiteness of the imagined north, and he remembers me, as I slip from one form to another, making space, giving up the ghost, choosing the continuity or otherwise. It is said that, if we are born again, we are born alone, forgetting, as we arrive, everything that has gone before - but who would have it otherwise? Who would wish to be accompanied into that first whiteness? The wind blows through us and we cannot choose what it remembers. All we can do is learn the shapes of the north, the shapes Bieggaålmaj makes crossing what once seemed a featureless landscape, far in the tundra, where only the mind is white, and the mind, like the land, goes on forever.

to hell with

JACOB POLLEY

DANDELIONS

For the time we have left and the times
we've asked the time of each other,
I pack you a weightless box of fluff, blown
from the roadside dandelion clocks.
Like an arrowhead or spear-tip,
I slip in a hollow-pointed pen nib
to say winter without you will be wordless,
the water coffined and the empty trees
unmoved by the wind as it moans.
Tell me what time it is. Tell me again.
I send you all I could recover
of those frail innumerable summer moons.

THE EGG

Don't leave the clothes pegs strung out along the line,
stand up straight or you'll buckle your spine,
chew each mouthful fifty times
and talk to no one taller than our back hedge!
But a pumpkin's too heavy for me
if I have to run away from the Egg.

October's last leaves are glued to the trees
when I step outside with the front-door key.
My friends are waiting for me
with their faces made up differently,
and what's the chance there's nothing to tell
but who'll marry money or run from the Egg?

On the street there's a snuffed-out-candle smell.
Cars edge the kerbs, their headlights cast like spells
to freeze and silence us. Doorbells
and letterboxes, the broken-into shed:
suddenly I'm all alone
at the locked park gates, ready to run from the Egg.

I won't share my breath with him.
I won't share my bones.
But dad's ironing shirts, my brother stayed in,
my mum sips brown ale while the blue sirens moan.
Milk, bananas, wholemeal bread:
whatever you're made of, you can't run from the Egg.

And someone comes closer, dragging footsteps,
dragging a shadow, holding his head,
and the moon's shaken out as darkness spreads
and the whites of his eyes overflow,
and my spine's bent back so it curls my toes
and my mouth's a loosened bow
and my mouth's a loosened bow

SARAH HALL

from BOTTLES

You liked being brought up where you were. Retrospectively, you're proud. It was rural and difficult and you feel accomplished now because of it. You think kids who have lived in the country are hardy that way; you think physicality and mentality coexist, that the region has made you durable and internally formidable. It's an obnoxious northern cliché, isn't it?

London is hard, but it's not that hard. It might be expensive and dirty and sometimes violent, it might have cultural clashes and water-shortages, but it's essentially micro-managed, nannied, coddled, monitored. Every street is video taped. Trains run to all corners of the metropolis and beyond. Someone will probably hear you choking if you are choking to death, or call the Police if you are being beaten to a pulp. There are amenities; dry-cleaners, groceries, post offices on every corner, well there used to be anyway, when you first moved here, a decade ago. Ambulances usually take only a few minutes to get to stroke victims. The safety net is tightly woven. All this stuff, about poverty, ghettos, dereliction, and drugs, the capital be all and end all, the here's where it's at, hub of the nation, the worst and most important suffering, is total and utter crap. London is spoiled, fawned-over, high-waged, glass-jawed.

The north of your youth was practically pre-industrial. Forget the idyll, the myths of the sublime, the pleasure ground. It was a question of filth loosened from fields, animal diseases, ringworms, drifts of snow, and long sickening bus rides to school. It was bad teeth, too many kids with disabilities, binge-drinking, black-eye Fridays, and badger baiting. It was about collecting wood off the fell and trying to keep it dry under tarpaulin so it didn't fizzle out green sap, hiss and blacken on the grate. Because that was how you stayed warm. No Economy 7. No piped gas. Pieces of fowl were strung from hooks in the out buildings by your neighbour, and in another shed trout was smoked. The heating range, which was plumbed in by your dad when you were fourteen to run some radiators, was bought off a local farmer. It was a cut-and-shunt boiler. It had been used to incinerate stillborn lambs. Your mother washed all the clothes by hand until that same year, when his paintings started fetching in some money, and a machine was bought and plumbed into the greasy, goose-hung bothy.

And when your friend Maggie collapsed from an asthma attack, she was airlifted to Newcastle Infirmary by helicopter, after forty-five minutes of lying under a witch-hazel bush, her brain bluely solidifying from the lack of oxygen. It was January. The black furrows were frozen and an earthy winter scent came off the ground - that smell of a struggle between minerals and the cold. You ran back from the phone box on the moor and wrapped Maggie in your coat and held her hand. This was the first and only time you've had to dial the emergency number. You waited for help, so insanely long, it seemed. Then the sky was ripped open by noise. You watched the SeaKing buzz down through sleet, and opened Maggie's mouth a fraction more because the wind from the propeller blades seemed strong enough to re-inflate her lungs. The witch-hazel carried pale orange flowers on its bare twigs, which looked almost impossible in the storm of the landing.

And that was that for Maggie. Deep Indefinite Unconsciousness. Coma. Technically, she is still alive. Officially, she was lucky. They got to her just in time to scrape up the last biological pat of her life off the hillside. No, it's not hard to associate the north with tragedy. And anyway, there's always half a truth to cliché, isn't there?

What you've been wondering about, what you really want to know, is when does it become apparent that somebody is truly lost to you?

For example. When is it likely that Maggie's family will give up hope and switch off the machines? She lies there, day after day, as she has for seventeen years, living by mechanical proxy, her hair as glossy as conkers, electrically retrograde behind her skull. You visit her often. You've got used to being chatty and fey, nothing but the sound of your own voice in the room and the soft flushing pipe of the ventilator. You tell her what is going on in the world, wondering if she has any notion of what year it is now. After the nurses leave her room you sometimes pass on gossip, secrets, personal titbits, the way you and she used to at school. The way best friends do. You whisper them down towards her ear. It's like making a confession to the oblivious ground, or blowing across the top of an empty bottle.

Her sisters send you Christmas cards each year on her behalf - the secretarial custodians of Maggie's half-life. How would they know if a week after The Decision was made, after they had brushed her hair and changed her nightie a last time, and told her goodbye we love you darling girl, hands one on top of each other over the circuit guard, how could they be sure this was not the week she was due to sit up finally, and ask what she got for her A level History, and say she fancied a rich tea biscuit, and wonder if her boyfriend Andy had been in to see her. Only to find out he had married her younger cousin, a year after Maggie went under. What is it that prevents them? You've never asked, nor will you.

The doctors measure her brain activity. From time to time there are electrical spikes, heat blooms. There's no way of knowing how aware she is, what she is hearing, what she is feeling and processing. The doctors say the green brain flares might be dreams. They say, don't dismiss her existence in case she is trapped within herself. Her spirit rattling around mutely, like a pea in a dead whistle.

People often respond oddly when they hear about Maggie. Nathan wanted to marry you. He asked very early on, four weeks in, in a café on Betterton Street, after you told him about her. There was a plate of marbled cheese on the table that you'd both been whittling knives through and you had a bottle of red wine on the go. He reached over and put his hands behind your neck, and in doing so caught a finger in your hair-band and pulled free your ponytail. It was an awkward moment. Your hair spilled forwards. Strange, the little things remembered. Downstairs, someone was giving a reading, a woman with an Uxbridge voice, and a whispering emphatic appreciation drifted up from the crowd after each poem.

You said no. Your reply was so unwavering that he has never asked again. Now and then you've wished he would. Either to say yes to. Or to instigate an ending.

He was hurt; you knew it. Still, you kept going out, regardless of the wind being knocked out of the fledgling romance. You kept cooking fresh pastas, sleeping against each other's backs, and then you moved in together. You upgraded from two shared suburban houses with fox-skunked gardens to one stylish sky-lit conservation-area flat. A great investment you were told at the time. The cast iron fireplace was ornamental but you always thought you might one day get it converted back to working order. You'd have bought coal from the garage. Or collected sticks off the heath, like the old nylon-bloused dears from your childhood village.

More than ever these days the flat seems to be on the brink of disaster, abandonment, though in reality it's perfectly secure. The mortgage goes out by standing order. Bills are managed. Laundry collects in a wicker hamper, and is washed. The floors are clean enough; you have one of those devices to sweep with, that magically attracts dust-bunnies. Ladles and spoons live in the second down of four fitted pine drawers, below a sophisticated granite counter. Everything between the walls is known, ordered, utilised.

But when you walk in through the door you feel the vague nausea of premonition, like it's the site of some kind of future conflict, the origin of quail-eyed refugees. Maybe this is all in your head, given your recent transgressions, your private knowledge of reckless activity. Over the last few weeks you haven't been spending much time there. You've been at the gallery, or out running on the heath; you've been going up north to see you mum and dad. You've been coming into the city for no real reason, not just on the days when you have appointments here, but just to be in motion, Just to get out, avoiding Nathan… Maybe.

In the beginning you felt connected to him, you really did. And you used him as a muse. You photographed him, sketched him, reproduced him, exposed him to the scrutiny of the public eye. He was good-humoured about your choices of anatomy. He seemed oblivious to the idea that his sexual organs would become delineated, hoisted up into the rafters of galleries or crucified to the wall by exploding masonry screws. He gave himself up gracefully.

He was happy to. You folded him over, opened his legs, let the lens remark upon the polished bronze flesh in his crevices, the brackish ghylls. He was the subject of your most successful and criticised series of compositions. Called *Bields*. You don't like that title now. Titles generally disappoint you, if that's not already obvious. You got so close in that gender become unidentifiable. The press went off about hermaphrodites, feminism, geo-portraiture.

You knew his display was better, more useable, for its lack of vanity, for its innocent kink.

Once you put him in your best tie-top stockings, Agent Provocateur. The hairs of his legs broke through the black mesh and his muscle definition gave the material a funerary look, like features blackly veiled. It excited both of you in a surprising way, and you went to bed and didn't speak through it but instead took turns doing whatever you wanted, with urgency and pragmatism.

The two of you are different now. Calmer. You have become good friends over the years. You've lost interest in seducing him, or being seduced. He no longer elicits your attention as a lover, not often. And then when it happens it's like assisted masturbation. You've stopped taking the pill. No need to bluff the flora of your reproductive system when it isn't being inundated with pollen, so to speak. You know him better as a housemate, a person who becomes gently furious at the news every evening, a great bread maker, a man who can't fry eggs. He knows you well, and has become, to an extent, a creature at your heels, with his eyes and hair and his predictive pace. He's one among the given number of human beings who fortify you. He's your familiar. A presence in proximity to all that you do.

You draw companionship from him, and stability, base nourishment, like chlorophyll absorbing light. All the powers you have for creativity and capriciousness, all the potency you wield - and you do wield it, via a Restoration palate of colour the reviewers have loved, a somewhat controversial agenda, dark sedge eyes, good legs, the ability to turn male heads on entering a room - are superfluous to the dynamic of the relationship now. His knowledge of you is assured, and limited. Your transactions are shallow. It's terrible to say it, but it's true.

You bring him tea every morning, comfort his headaches with paracetamol, you are generous with birthday presents. But disclosure of your self is frugal. The frisson is gone. He lives on the scraps, the affection, as if it's enough. But how could it be, for a red-blooded male? There's no entitlement to your body anymore, granted through sheer arduous solicitation, an obvious hard-on as you undress. No mascara is applied solely for him. No sexy lingerie is worn to thrill. Now you wear it to work instead, the silk dampening, the stiff lace cuffs chafing you under your dresses.

Your mind tracks to someone else when you touch yourself. You turn over memories of the recent muted sex you've had in rooms where there was too little space, this other man's ecstatic repression because he is only able to reach for you sometimes, because it is illicit, and there are prohibitions. You leave the room where Nathan sits reading or humming over Soduku, go to the bathroom; you lean forward on the cold mirror, feel down inside your bra, unfasten however many buttons on your jeans you need to. In your mind you are elsewhere. In your mind you have disconnected from Nathan. But, then, you aren't making any physical moves to leave him.

The night he was in Birmingham, when you brought this other man home, was not the first night of unfaithfulness. You'd been with him before. He works at Borwood House too. Not as a curator or employee exactly. He's translating a journal loaned for the exhibition, a freelance commission for the project, as well as using the place for his own writing, like a lavish Victorian office. This is how you have become close. This is how you have had the opportunity to.

Five weeks ago, out of the blue, you went into the back room of the gallery and leaned over his table and kissed the back of his neck. You felt a rush of chemical gold in your head and in your chest as he made a soft-throated noise, in enjoyment. He put his hands on the sides of the chair, like he was sitting on a rock in fast water, holding

on firmly. There was no premeditation to your actions, but then it
felt like there was no other option or course to be taken. Which
sounds like an excuse, you know.

It was just one of those times when your faculties seem irrelevant.
When automatic pilot takes over. Or opportunism. He was in the
space you occupied. His form. His scent. You hadn't really talked
much since he started working at Borwood, but you were conscious
of his presence in your territory. That day, you were more conscious
than ever, and you tracked him down. You let your damp teeth rest
against the side of his throat, with instinctive and natural precision,
as if issuing some kind of feral warning. Your lips moved humidly
towards his mouth and you kissed him. He complied. He opened his
mouth, brought your tongue inside with the tip of his own. And a
new dimension suddenly opened for you both also.

He stood up, and told you he liked your outfit, as if that mattered.
Then he became serious and said he was so sorry about your
brother's death. He remembered meeting Danny last autumn,
they'd got through half a bottle of whisky together in the Academy
club after the Farenholtz showing, and Danny had ended up passing
out on his couch.

Your eyes stung, brightened with emotion. You looked at his mouth,
still glazed with wetness from your own, and his softened brow. His
facial expression conveyed an assurance that he thought these
words would halt the proceedings, and an accompanying
disappointment that was lovely, moving. And there was something
else in him. Compassion. There was absolute compassion in his face,
like nobody else had managed to express yet about the accident. It
reminded you of a closeness you once had, years ago, and how it felt
to be in-separate, compatible with someone else.

You stepped towards him again. You pushed him down on the desk,
unzipped his trousers. You kept him in your mouth even at the end
when he tried to gain polite release from you before coming. It was
easy. It was inexcusable.

to hell with

KEVIN CUMMINS

TOOTING TIM

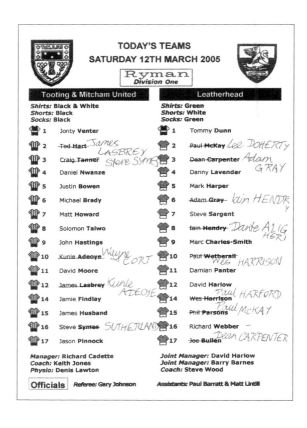

Go on yeah go on go on oh oh go on Sol oh Tooting Tooting Tooting Tooting Tooting I fell asleep on the train guess where I fucking ended up fucking Leatherhead Precious Precious he's into rambling and he's into buggery Precious Precious come on you stripes come on you stripes unlucky fucking hell unlucky they've got a few yeah no yeah er no they're not for any particular part of the ground the thing is come on Tooting come on Tooting come on Tooting come on Tooting I'm quite happy going behind the goal yeah got to make sure we're all standing in the same place did quite well at their place make sure we're all together make sure of that come on you stripes come on you stripes Mitcham Mitcham you jammy sod bloody hell pick 'em up pick 'em up man come on Tooting come on Tooting come on Tooting pillage the village the referee was a prick they've got an identical record yeah right yeah oh come on Hastings was behind the defender when the other fella blocked it sing when you're farming sing when you're farming hold it Mitcham Mitcham Mitcham Mitcham Mitcham Mitcham Mitcham Mitcham Mitcham Mitcham go on great tackle oh fucking hell ref that's a free kick now ref go with him that's well won come on Tooting come on Tooting come on Tooting come on Tooting come on Tooting keep up with the play referee get off you village idiot get back to your field you village idiot come on you stripes come on you stripes Tooting Tooting Tooting Tooting Tooting Tooting we're the Bog End we're the Bog End we're the Bog End Sandy Lane who's challenging go go go go go go yeah yeah yeah oh Tooting Tooting Tooting Tooting Tooting Tooting yeah good one Tooting Tooting Tooting Tooting Tooting Tooting Tooting Terrors Terrors Terrors Terrors that was fucking awful another classic Tooting set piece how about getting the ball in the box once in a while oh get up you tart yeah oh fuck off fuck off what a load of bollocks yeah Matty you wanker fucking wanker come on that's a typical whinging farmer fucking hurray aargh oh well played free kick ref he's fucking all over the place how long is it going to be before you blow up you idiot get on him eh you take it ref ref in your own time come on you stripes come on you stripes piss off go on oh for fuck's sake keep possession Tooting keep it on the ground we hate Dulwich we hate Dulwich we hate Dulwich we hate Dulwich hold it up good good unlucky come on Tooting come on Tooting come on Tooting come on Tooting come on Tooting come on you stripes come on you stripes come on that's another fine harvest offside oh fucking hell ref Tooting Tooting Tooting Tooting think about it oh fucking hell they don't want to know come on pick him up James he's your man we argh farmer you're fucking having a laugh lino come on lino come on Johnny Hastings we yeah yeah yeah fucking yeah United United United great header though he wasn't favourite to get it either Wayne Cort scoring with a header fucking hell oh no great challenge great challenge well played good recovery Chin concentrate Matty corner come on Tooting come on Tooting come on Tooting come on Tooting oh fuck off every fucking time he does that going yeah where's he going it's in the back yeah Tooting Tooting Tooting in the box come on let's have a challenge argh go on oooooooooooh come on you stripes come on you stripes he's on his own just hold him up hold him up oh you're joking leave it leave it leave the referee to us fucking farming collaborator what a load of bollocks referee piss off get back to your farming what a load of bollocks referee yokel collaborator oh fuck off referee fuck off go Daniel get out of that yeah he lost it yeah come on Tooting come on Tooting come on Tooting oh fucking hell ref fuck off back to Nuremberg easy ten yards go on the ten men argh off off off off off off off off off off off that's a real foul referee that's what you should be worrying about you plonker that's a real foul that last defender ref piss off yea yeah yeah fuck off cheerio cheerio cheerio cheerio cheerio cheerio cheerio cheerio cheerio he'd already got away with quite a bit come on send the whinging farmers off farm army farm army come on Tooting come on Tooting come on Tooting come on Tooting don't talk don't talk to the ref leave him to us in the back in the back if you got your stomach out of your eyes ref you'd have seen the in the back Brady's experience shows I don't mind the odd psycho challenge but he's been ok really since he came back why is that not a foul if he plays the man it's a foul ref where's he taking it if he moves it any further Jesus Christ ref he's in Morden oh fucking hell ref donkey look at that fucking it was more of a foul on Stevie Symes he hardly touched him he didn't give that it certainly should have been I take it you can buy a ticket for anywhere in the ground then let it go Dan fucking hell get up Lumpy our ball what about that you donkey no that was a typical Jonty pass that one head up Justin come on Tooting where's he taking it ref it wasn't that bad a ball come on what about the stealing from the throw fucking hell get it up Jonty that's more like it go on go on come on put a bit of pressure on a bit of aggression Wayne he should be shitting himself with you charging at him yeah go on go on go on go on he's there oh no no way lino he didn't look offside to me he had a dreadful game on Tuesday where to pick 'em up Tooting concentrate aaaaarrrrrr my watch has suddenly gone five minutes slow well I think my watch has suddenly become slow that'll do that's a good knock Wayne put him under keep going Wayne stop good head play safe don't fuck around ooh that's a shit tackle with ten against ten we were saying that Brady was the man for the time well you can't have one bit of him without the other it seems he's always been he's always been a good player at his best and diabolical at his worst where they taking these throws from that's good cover well done Justin er Daniel dreadful throw out you cunt Jonty it's a bit panicky come on Tooting he's holding him get involved Wayne get involved fucking imbecile that's better well played well played distribution tackling everything's got to improve second half distribution Tooting well out that's well played get there first Wayne 'kin' 'ell he's nowhere near it he's scored a goal he thinks he's done his bit for the day he plays better when he's not scoring I think sometimes come on Tooting come on Tooting come on Tooting go on get that away well played go on Matty yeah wooooah well done and again Justin come on second ball Tooting you're fucking hanging around you want to go up the fucking side for it it's got to be a Tooting ball how can you moan about that what the fuck is going on don't they practice come on Tooting come on Tooting come on Tooting get some fucking lift on the ball it's like watching a bunch of five year olds with our free kicks go on go on go on that's good that's better oh you cunt they want to concentrate the effort spent on dissent into winning the ball aaaaaarrrr bloody hell we should have had a free kick for that keep battling Tooting you're fucking woeful ref it wasn't even a foul it was we won't get out of the league on this sort of performance (Half Time) yeah oh no Mitcham Mitcham Mitcham Mitcham Mitcham come on Tooting come on in you go Nwanze that's well in oh fucking hell that's better Steve come on that's good that's good yeah he had a great game against er Hastings play to the whistle Tooting yeah against Johnno come on Tooting come on Tooting come on Tooting come on Tooting that's encouraging referee wake up you wanker take your time Jonty it looked like he was being get involved fucking hell Tooting ball I like it get in Solomon gotta improve on this though get the fucking ball come on Tooting lift it we're better than this we miss Kinchy don't waste time on the fucking referee fucking hell we've lost the ball hold him up hold him up go on win it win it fucking get in and fucking win it fucking pansying around fucking wanker this is comparable to the Barking game really Tooting Tooting Tooting Tooting Tooting fucking hell Jonty kick the ball fucking hell Jonty kick the ball win it win it win it saved Jonty go away fuck off come on you stripes come on you stripes fucking hell well he give it perfect challenge that by Cort er yeah Barking yeah a disaster that game at Barking yeah 'cos er Tanner he got booked first then he got injured come on let's have some consistency with those throws not too bad oh fuck off again oh no no go on it's a lovely ball get in get the fucking ball Lumpy play as if you mean it they pissed all over us in the game over there and we beat them three one it's a foul throw it's a foul throw referee second half they were all over us but we just happened to be three nil up get involved hold it up don't lose it oh fuck it's a load of bollocks it's the other way if anything a load of bollocks referee got someone coming off you're wrong referee are you claiming that ref well played ref you can claim that it's your goal ref wanker come on Tooting pull your finger out there's a relegation side out there at the moment Tooting Tooting Tooting Tooting should have put the reserves in against

Barking and er come on Tooting come on Tooting come on Tooting well they're not holding the ball up but I mean that the last time Matt does a good job he gets fucking penalised and they score a goal get the ball moving again oh fucking hell what's he fucking doing distribution and tactics well in Justin come on fucking get stuck in and start passing the ball Mitcham Mitcham Mitcham Mitcham Mitcham Mitcham Mitcham fucking raise your game his skill's non-existent not for the first time referee oh you wanker he had the fucking ball fucking hell ref get on the far post ref unlucky ref you fucking cheat if we don't get decisions like that we've got no chance we're playing badly enough as it is without the fucking ref giving them every 50/50 oh referee you're fucking come on referee you fucking cheat referee every fucking time against Leatherhead they put the worst referee you yokel collaborator fucking bunch of fucking wankers that's better Justin we try to play football with the odd exception unlucky unlucky get up Matty James watch the fucking game ball watching or what good challenge well recovered wanker you're fucking having a laugh you wanker he wasn't standing there you wanker that was abysmal referee wakey wakey come on referee get up this pitch get your stomach out of your eyes you useless git I don't believe this if you've got the chance to cross the ball fucking cross it Lumpy pansying around oh fucking fuck off get involved come on Tooting come on Tooting take your time fucking hell another fucking famous fucking Tooting set piece go on come on you stripes come on Tooting come on Tooting Nwanze show some fucking urgency in the air that's ok good challenge we'll have that referee let's have some justice here Matty oh fucking hell why don't you fucking take it ref you fucking wanker get in the wall ref come on the ten men you fucking waste of skin referee you useless tosser that's fucking class bit late to start evening it up now ref come on Tooting come on Tooting that's better off off off no I don't think he'll do it how about the ten yards you tart put it in Matty come on Tooting come on Tooting come on Tooting come on Tooting ten yards come on that's not ten yards nowhere near what about the ten yards how can we fucking score with a wall that far back he was never going to get the ball in with a wall that far back you can't get it up and round them hammer it low I expect I don't know why they didn't let Matty take the free kick he's got a track record of scoring or hitting the post with the free kick I don't think we'll get much after that one that's well won make it Wayne come on Tooting come on Tooting come on Tooting well played Solomon that's a almost a good ball come on Stevie take him on take him all the way how's he fouling he's got the fucking ball to be fair if anything I thought that last free kick he gave us was pretty mysterious as well the ref was in a better position than the linesman to see it be interesting to see what he does with the ten yards that's not ten he didn't pace it corner come on Tooting come on Tooting come on Tooting sing when you're farming go on go on John

oh bollocks wasn't a bad ball didn't see that lino did ya I actually
thought we'd started improving then no there's no shape about the side
we're very thin in midfield without Kinchy come on Tooting come on
Tooting come on Tooting get behind them careful go on Matty unlucky
he was off it was a really late flag though come on Nwanze Mitcham
come on Tooting squeeze the man let's use the wind for a change come
on you stripes come on you stripes come on come on Johnno fuck fuck
off unlucky Tooting where'd he take it from good head Justin it's a Tooting
ball come on Tooting come on Tooting come on Tooting no way that's
in unlucky keep going Sol keep going Sol oh you tosser played Nwanze
time Johnny Hastings unlucky should have done better there he saw
the gap but he didn't quite find it well in Lazzer go on Wayne hold it up
a bit more fucking get stuck in come on Matty that's in come on well
played John Hastings keep going Wayne come on come on Tooting
come on Tooting come on Tooting he's getting all angry relatively
speaking we had half an attack there he covered two players there
Lasbury to be fair fucking hell the unexploded bomb or a bit of an
unexploded bomb there unlucky there he defended it well there I think
it fell to him quite nicely fucking hell he scored from a goal kick once
well I think the player jumped into him a little there come on John
actually it's been the midfield that's been the real problem go on Matty
he's getting into the game a bit more go on one more one more ooooh
unlucky go on Matty that's it come on Tooting come on Tooting come
on Tooting come on Tooting nick one go on ooooooh shit well played
Justin come on you stripes super super John super super John super
super John super Johnny Hastings hit hit hit the fucking thing hit the
fucker take responsibility good effort come on hit the ball Lumpy come
on don't be afraid to shoot Tooting it was criminal that by Lumpy I mean
what's he going to do by bringing the ball down with defenders right on
top of him that's it that's good that's better come on John come on Matty
arrrrgh referee referee keep up with the play fucking hell referee get up
with the play referee you fat cunt go aaaar fucking blatant shirt-pulling
you useless tosser of a referee come on Tooting come on Tooting
come on Tooting come on Tooting played Steve that's alright go on it's
absolutely ridiculous that a ref makes that he pushed him then he
pulled his shirt that's a dreadful ball what're you trying to achieve with
that fucking hospital ball take it on Lazza yes he was fouled ref first time
he's spotted anything this ref oh fuck come on John win it that's alright
that's alright too come on Matty come on Tooting come on Tooting come
on Tooting come on Tooting come on Tooting come on you stripes come
on you stripes well played corner corner Steve might get a touch here
it's worth a shout come on you stripes come on you stripes fucking get
the cunt over great ball Lumpy lovely ball that's the one in the back
fucking hell referee come on Stevie it's there aaarrgh it was a great header
by Stevie Symes there yeah come on Tooting come on Tooting come

on Tooting it's in the back referee wakey wakey well in Solomon that's well won Solomon and again well played Johnny Hastings Mitcham Mitcham Mitcham Mitcham Mitcham Mitcham Hastings played well apart from that finish he works hard go on that's good go on hit one fucking hell take responsibility go on Lumpy that's well played go on Matty his finishing was poor on Tuesday but it's worse today I'd like to see Kunle on for a little bit oh fucking hell well played John unlucky well worked Kunle Kunle oh fucking hell another Nuremburg idiot it's fucking outrageous referee the referee wan't even watching go on Kunle go on Kunle aargh referee fucking hell played Justin fucking holding him there he had the arm on his shoulder there must be time Mitcham Mitcham Mitcham Mitcham it's been better the last twenty minutes Terrors Terrors Terrors Terrors Terrors fucking hell don't do anything fancy just kick the ball long come on you stripes come on you stripes trouble foul referee fucking cheat referee you wanker you fucking idiot referee get your stomach out of your eyes you useless tosser hope you're pleased with that one referee a fucking disgrace free kick against the wind fat fucking advantage that is Mitcham Mitcham Mitcham Mitcham Mitcham come on Tooting come on Tooting come on Tooting get him off Kunle that's a lovely ball Lumpy fucking hell unlucky he bottled it should have fucking got that ball over he should have done oh what a surprise he fell over his own feet it was minimal Tooting Tooting Tooting that was a nothing free kick that's trouble you fucking cheat the linesman gave it the other way it's not your fucking decision you fat cunt get on the back post ref get the fucking ball don't panic don't pan oh you silly cunt you don't have to dive in you berk he ain't going nowhere fucking five year olds playing out there it wasn't there either referee that's your goal your goal referee it's your fucking goal it's the referee's goal your goal referee you wanker that's your goal over-rule the fucking linesman that's your goal we never cleared it from that corner what's Nwanze doing what kind of fucking defending is that come on Tooting come on Tooting c'mon get a fucking challenge in get involved get involved Lumpy that was basically down to the referee over-ruling the linesman come on c'mon get involved you fucking cheat referee you wanker fucking cheat the referee's a wanker the referee's a wanker the referee's a wanker you fucking cheat referee

to hell with

WILLY VLAUTIN

GRANDSON

The meeting was in twenty five minutes and the woman, Nora Robinson, sat at her kitchen table nervously drinking ice tea and watching the clock on the stove. Five minutes more passed and she stood, went to the bathroom one last time, and looked herself over. Her hair was brown and gray and pulled back in a bun. Her skirt was black and she wore a blue sweater and a small necklace that her daughter had given her years before. She fixed her lipstick and stepped back.

She had gained thirty pounds in the year since she'd last seen her daughter, where she'd talked too much, where she'd said what she'd said. She tried to pull the sweater down, tried to arrange the skirt, but nothing would hide it, she'd gotten fat and that was it.

As she made the drive to her daughter's she told herself to say whatever was necessary, to do whatever was necessary to see her grandson, see his face for the first time.

Her daughter, the boyfriend, and the baby lived together in a one bedroom apartment on the bottom floor of a rundown one hundred unit complex. She parked on the street, found a stick of gum in her purse, and got out of the car.

She walked to the door and as she did her breath tightened and her nerve began to disappear. There were cars on blocks in the parking lot, there were Mexican men standing around drinking beer, barbecuing. There were kids playing in the small dirt courtyard.

She knocked on the door.

Her daughter answered.

"You made it," the girl said.

"Of course," Nora said and was let in.

The apartment inside was in disarray. There were clothes strewn about the living room, on the floor, and on the couch. There was a large entertainment center and on it a TV with a talk show going on.

Her daughter set herself in a recliner and changed the channel on the TV with the remote.

"Where's Miguel?" Nora asked.

"He's out."

"No, I mean Miguel Junior, the baby. I'm so excited to finally see him."

"He's in the bedroom," the girl said.

"Can we see him?"

"I want to finish my program first."

Her mother sat on the couch across from her. "How have you been?" She asked.

"Aunt April came over last week and saw the baby."

"I heard."

"What did you hear?"

"Nothing. She just called and told me how cute the baby was."

"What, you didn't think he would be cute?"

"Of course I thought he'd be cute. I can't wait to see him."

"He's still half Mexican."

"Look, I'm sorry about what I said. It was a long time ago and I feel horrible about it. You know I do. I didn't mean what you think I meant. It just came out sounding that way. I was just worried when you quit calling home. That's all. I didn't know what to think."

"I had a lot going on," the daughter said.

"I'm hoping I can make it up to you. After all these years, after all you've been through, after all we've been through, you know we can work this out."

"I have nothing to work out. You're the one who doesn't like Mexicans. You're the one that hates anyone south of the border."

"I've never had a problem with that. I've never had a problem with Mexicans. You know why I was worried. You know why and it had nothing to do with who you were dating and what race he was."

The daughter got up and went to the kitchen, took a two liter bottle of soda from the fridge, and poured herself a glass.

Nora watched from the couch. Her daughter, just twenty years old, had gained weight herself. Fifty maybe sixty pounds. She was dressed in gray sweat pants and a black T-shirt. Her hair was long and brown and held back in a pony tail. Her eyebrows were shaved and penciled in. She had three tattoos on her left hand.

She came back to the recliner and again began turning the channels on the TV.

"Have you been working?" Nora asked.

"I don't have too. Miguel takes care of me. He takes care of everything."

"That's wonderful," she said. "You must be happy to get to stay home with the baby."

"I'm not lazy if that's what you're asking."

"I would never say that. You know I'd never say that," Nora said.

The girl went back to watching the TV.

"I'm still at the power company," she tried again. "I just hit twenty years if you can believe that."

"No wonder you don't know anything," her daughter said.

"Hey, come on that's not fair. Look, I can see you're angry with me, and I'm sorry for that. I really am. It was a misunderstanding what I said. You know it was. Deep down you must know that. I've tried to be a good mother to you. When you got in trouble those times who helped you out? Who nursed you back to health, who paid for your counselling, who visited you every day at the treatment center?"

"I knew you were going to bring that up."

"You're my daughter," she said in desperation. "I love you. I wanted to help. I wasn't trying to put you down. I just want you to know that I'm here for you. I know I've made mistakes, and I apologize for them. I just want to be a part of your life. Can't you see? I'm here, I'm trying."

"He doesn't need a grandmother. Miguel's sister takes him when I want her to."

"I'd love to meet her. I'd like to meet any of his family. I would. I'm not a horrible person."

"You're a carpet, mom. People just walk over you. They always have. Listen to yourself."

"You're my daughter," Nora said and tears began to well in her eyes.

In the distance, in the bedroom, the baby began to cry.

"Is that him?" Nora asked finally.

"Who else would it be?"

"Can I go back and see him?"

"I haven't made up my mind yet," the daughter said.

"I'm trying," Nora said. "I really am trying. I don't know what else to do."

"Say you're a racist," her daughter said finally. "If you want to see my son I want you to say, 'I'm a racist white bitch that doesn't know shit about anything. I answer phones for the power company.'"

"You want me to say that?"

"If you want to see your grandson I want you to say it."

"Why would you do this to me?"

"If you don't want to say it, you know where the door is."

Nora paused for a moment and wiped the tears from her eyes.

"Okay," she said but her voice began to fail her. "I'm a racist white bitch that doesn't know shit."

"What else?"

"I can't remember what else you said."

"Say 'I answer phones for the power company, that's all I'll ever be.' Say the whole thing."

"I don't know what I did that was so wrong."

"If you want to see my son, you say it."

"Alright, I'm a racist white bitch that doesn't know shit. I answer phones for the power company, that's all I'll ever be."

"He's in the room," her daughter said with her eyes focused on the TV.

Nora stood up. Her legs shook and she could barely stand. It was all she could do not to break down in tears on the floor, to crumble and collapse. She stepped over the clothes and the magazines and walked to the bedroom where the cries of the baby grew louder and more frequent the closer she came.

The baby lay in a crib in the bedroom. His face was red from crying. The air in the room was stale and smelled of dirty diapers and cigarette and marijuana smoke. The bed was unmade and clothes lay all around the floor. There was a large TV that sat on milk crates and it was turned on. There was a bong on the night stand and a stack of videos. She picked up the boy and held him, and when she did, his crying slowly stopped. She whispered to him and he stared at her. She looked around the room and could see her reflection in a large mirror that hung behind the bed. It was true she really was going gray and her face looked tired and wrinkled, her back hurt, and her hands were becoming arthritic. She was old. She didn't know if she could be a mother again if it ended that way. If she got the call some night or a knock at the door some morning. But she'd try, she'd have to. She held the boy and took deep breaths.

"Oh little boy, what's going to become of you," she said softly to him.

to hell with

CLARE WIGFALL

SAFE

They started to disappear in February. The first in a shopping centre in Leeds, right beneath the watch of a security camera. One moment there was a baby, strapped in its carriage as the mother leant to look in the window of a shop selling sports shoes; the next moment, gone. Just like that. As if someone had spliced the camera film.

Standing alone, the case was unexplained, yet still unextraordinary. It was only after a pattern started to appear – a fourth baby disappearing without trace – that the Leeds CCTV footage made the national news.

After that, there were two more in one week. One from a park in Edinburgh, another from a hospital ward in Hull. Then two from private homes which reported all doors and windows locked. And then came the case in Hampshire with the moving car.

The Chief of Police made a statement. He stood for the cameras before the revolving blue sign of New Scotland Yard and instructed the public not to panic. 'Distressing as these incidents are,' he reasoned, his voice so confident, so reassuring, 'our best teams of investigators are working round the clock to find a rational explanation. I am confident we will be returning these infants safely to their parents in no time at all.'

But the very next night news reports were covering another case, a thirty-something couple from North London whose three-month-old had vanished from her sleepcot.

'Another one?' asked Lella from the doorway.

'Yeah.'

She stood there, on her way up to the bathroom, and instinctively lowered her head to kiss her own baby's crown. Above the milken smell of skin, she paused, her eyes fixed on the couple on the television screen.

'These ones, they look like people like us,' she said.

He made no response.

'It's weird though, isn't it? Makes it seem more…kind of real, you know what I mean?'

'Cause you can't imagine people like them doing their own baby in?'

'I didn't say that.' Her eyes pulled from the television screen. 'That's horrible to even think something like that.'

'It's probably what's happening.'

'You don't know anything.' She turned upstairs to run a bath for the baby.

'Lella,' she heard him cry after her, 'I didn't mean- Lell'-.'

Locking the door behind her, Lella turned on both the taps.

While she was cleaning the kitchen counter the following morning, her j-cloth swept up three small, blackened scraps, like charred grains of rice. She stopped, and lifted one between her rubber-gloved fingers to study it.

Mouse droppings, was the realisation that came suddenly. Mice. She threw a quick glance about the kitchen, as if she might locate the culprit immediately. But of course there was only herself and the baby, sleeping contentedly in the baby seat sat in the middle of the room. Lella swept the other two scraps into her hand and disposed of them in the bin, then sprayed the whole countertop again with cleaning fluid and wiped it down, wondering if they sold mousetraps in Sainsbury's.

In the following week, three more babies went missing. The police urged new parents to be vigilant. When she was out now, Lella couldn't help noticing the concerned looks people would give her as she passed with the baby carriage.

'It's okay,' she wanted to smile back at them, 'I'm keeping her safe.'

But the more they replayed on television the CCTV footage of that first Leeds baby that had gone missing, the one that appeared to just vanish from its carriage as the young mother paused to look in a shop window, the more Lella felt uncomfortable each time she laid the baby in the ergonomic all-terrain carriage they'd purchased at such great expense. It made her nervous to have the baby out of her view as she pushed. And she wasn't the only one, she realised, after she had to try three baby shops before she could find one that hadn't sold out of baby slings.

'Keep 'em close to you this way,' said the shop assistant, as she swiped Lella's credit card. 'Can't be too safe right now, can you?'

On the radio that afternoon, there was a discussion about the disappearances that Lella was listening to as she fed the baby. Or half-listening, anyway. She kept dropping off, then she'd open her eyes again and once more catch the thread of the discussion, cradling the baby's head with her palm. 'You're hungry today, little girl,' Lella smiled, sleepy from broken nights. Her breasts felt tender. A psychologist was talking about the impact current events were having on the national psyche. The baby made a snuffling sound and clasped its hand around one of Lella's fingers. It was one of the first spring days, and the window was open. Not too wide, because Lella was worried about the baby catching a chill from the draught, but it felt good to let fresh air into the room after the winter months.

'People need to feel safe,' the psychologist was saying, 'they need to feel they can protect,' and that was when Lella heard the noise. A muffled shuffling and scratching. She cocked her head and listened. It was very faint, but she was sure she could hear something. Reaching over, she turned off the radio, still listening. A sound like crumpled newspaper being rustled together, and then a panicky gnawing, coming from the wall behind her, low down. Gently, she drew the baby from her breast, laid her on the sofa cushion beside her, and snapped back her bra. The baby started to cry. 'Shh,' hushed Lella, her ear still listening for that new sound. She went behind the sofa and lowered herself on her knees beside the wall. The sound was more strong here; a scritchy, persistent sound. Out of her sight, the baby let out another small wail. 'Shh,' said Lella again, as she rested her ear against the wall.

There was definitely something there. Something alive.

Lella was not the kind of woman to be disturbed by rodents. She'd never had a problem with them. But that had been when they were pets, kept in cages that were cleaned regularly, with coloured plastic tube mazes to climb through and wheels to run in. She was aware now that whatever was making the noise was just inches away from her on the inside of the wall, and the realisation made her body chill suddenly, like everything was shrinking up inside herself. Very slowly, as if she didn't want to disturb whatever it was, she rose again and turned back to the sofa.

Breeze billowed the pale curtain as Lella felt her heart leap and her throat gag with a horrible sick-making shock. There was the baby, lying on the cushion, sucking at its fist in place of Lella's nipple, and right beside it was the open window. Anyone could have just leant in.

She told her husband that night. 'I think we have mice.'

'Mice?'

'I've found droppings. And today I heard them in the living room wall.'

'In the walls? It's more likely rats in London.'

'Please don't say that,' she shuddered, smiling as she poured more wine into his glass.

'Call Rentokil.'

'I did. They said they were experiencing unusually high custom and put me on hold. I waited twenty minutes then gave up. We're missing the news,' she said, glancing at the clock, but as she stood he caught her round the waist and pulled her towards him. For a few moments they embraced.

'You seem a bit better today,' he said.

'Maybe.'

'Let's have an early night,' he whispered against her middle, but as he did he felt her body tense and pull back from him.

'The doctor said wait six weeks, you know that,' she said sharply and twisted from his embrace.

She worried when the baby was out of her sight now. When she used the bathroom, she took the baby in with her. When she showered, she left the curtain pulled slightly back so she could see her on the bath mat. She took her into bed with them and held her close, her back turned to her husband in case he rolled over in his sleep. She would check herself if even just for a moment she turned her back on the baby whilst in a room with her.

Because that was all it took, a second of inattention. She kept hearing the desperate parents on the news programmes say so, recall how they'd just glanced away for a second, and when they looked back their babies were gone. Vanished into thin air. That's what they kept saying through their sobs. 'I just got up to switch on the television, and when I looked back he was gone. Vanished into thin air.' Only the night before she heard a story like that on the radio. And as she listened, the thought that came to Lella's mind was, 'They couldn't have loved them enough.' She knew it wasn't fair to think this way, but she couldn't banish her belief; 'If they loved them as much as I love my baby, they wouldn't have lost them.'

Eighty-three had now gone missing. A huge number. A number that could no longer be explained away in any rational manner. A number that was perplexing and horrifying the nation. It made no sense. The police still claimed to be optimistic, but they hadn't solved a single case. They hadn't found a single baby. Not even the body of a baby. Each further day they remained unfound, the tension in the country was rising.

Lella focused on the faces of the parents in the newspapers, as if in their expressions she might find some clue everyone else was missing. She stared at the baby photos, the rows of missing babies that all started to look alike after a while, and pulled her own baby close against her chest.

'You should stop reading the news,' said her husband, coming into the kitchen to find her poring over an article, the radio playing by her elbow. 'It's not healthy to be obsessing over it so much. Thinking about these things isn't going to help you.'

'What do you know?' she asked him angrily, then regretted it and let him put his arms around her.

She saw it the next day, whilst she was sitting in the living room feeding the baby. A swift sleek black shape scurrying along the skirting board to disappear into the hallway. So fast that for a second she thought she was hallucinating. She gasped, and the movement shook the baby from her breast. It began to whimper softly, but Lella was still too stunned to react. The creature had been so big. Definitely not a mouse. Bigger than she'd even imagined a rat would be. Yet it must have been a rat, because the image that replayed now in her mind was the movement of the tail curling out of the doorframe. A thick pink tail, like uncooked sausage meat.

This time she remained on the line when they put her on hold. Over forty-five minutes she waited.

'Four weeks at the earliest,' said the woman.

'You can't send someone for four weeks?'

'We've been inundated with calls. There's a nation-wide epidemic.'

'I saw in the newspaper, but-'

'I'm really sorry,' said the woman. 'There's nothing I can do. Don't leave any food out. Keep your rubbish bags tied up. We'll send someone as soon as we can.'

'But I have a baby,' said Lella.

The woman paused. 'I'm sorry,' she said.

Lella didn't want to tell her husband, but she was rarely leaving the house these days. She knew the baby was just as vulnerable inside the house, but it felt safer this way. Going outdoors made her nervous. She was jumpy, shied away each time somebody came near her.

Exhaustion didn't help. Each night she would lie in the dark, feeling the baby's shallow breath against her neck as she focused blearily on the pattern in the wallpaper or the blinking digits of the clock radio, terrified by the shadows but frightened to close her eyes and lose contact. Instead, her body forced sleep upon her by day, grabbing at it greedily as she sat feeding or reading the paper. Each time, she would be jolted from unconsciousness again with a jerk of terror as her mind remembered the baby and panicked wildly for a moment before she realised she was lying safe in her arms.

She didn't want her husband to know she wasn't leaving the house any longer because he'd only worry for her more. She feared he might bring up the idea of a counsellor again. So she was clever about it, and congratulated herself that this was a secret that wasn't so difficult to keep from him. By telephone, she set up an account with the newsagent to have the paper delivered each day. The shopping could be ordered online and delivered to the door. She fabricated visits to friends. It all could be managed. She'd even ordered rat poison online.

Babies were still disappearing. The computerised maps of the country that played on the news each night sprouted more and more cases until they looked like the pincushion her mother used to keep in the sewing chest, each coloured dot marking another missing baby.

She'd taken to wearing the baby in the sling even as she did the housework. It felt safer this way, feeling her close. It was while she was cleaning one of the kitchen cabinets that she found the nest.

The first thing she noticed was tiny scraps of chewed paper, and then a spill of flour and lentils that had escaped from their packages. When she pushed these aside, there at the back of the cupboard she saw a greyish mass of paper and fluff. Like a tiny blanket she might have made as a child for her dolls. She bent lower, careful not to bump the baby, and reached forward with a rubber-gloved hand to slide it towards her.

With a scream, Lella fell back from the cupboard onto her rear. She scooted backwards across the floor, and at her chest the baby's voice rose in a thin wail. Breathing heavily, Lella leant against the oven door, her legs still sprawled across the kitchen floor, the baby screeching. Her heart was beating in her eardrums. She sat like this for a few minutes, and when she'd eventually calmed a little she crawled forward again on her knees and peered into the cupboard to take another look in the grey nest.

At first she'd thought they were maggots, or worms writhing, but she could see now that what had so surprised her were ten or so baby rats wriggling over and about each other. They were each only about an inch and a half long, a little thinner than her thumb, and perfectly pink. Their flesh hung wrinkled, as if too big for their bodies. Their eyes were still just dark smudges beneath the skin, and their ears not yet distinct from their heads. Their arms and legs were scrabbling, the toes still undefined. Only the tails seemed advanced, almost as thick as their bodies and pink. The small creatures wriggled blindly in the nest, the sight of them turning Lella's stomach.

Breaking her initial paralysis, she grabbed for the tea towel and wrapped it loosely about the nest so she could lift it. Rising from the floor, she held the bundle gingerly before her, hushing her howling baby as she stepped quickly up the stairs to the bathroom. Before she could allow herself to give it a second thought, she released the towel over the toilet bowl, and watched the tiny pink creatures and the mass of paper and fluff drop. The baby rats were flapping their legs in the water. Horrified, Lella slammed down the lid and pressed the flush. The water gushed, and she stood there, listening until the cistern had fully filled again, then flushed once more before she lifted the toilet lid. The toilet bowl was again empty, the water clear.

Lella dropped suddenly to her knees, and with a violence that frightened her vomited up everything in her stomach. The baby was whimpering, pressed as it was against her thighs and the cold ceramic of the toilet bowl.

Eventually, when Lella could retch no more, she collapsed onto the bathroom floor and curled against the bathtub sobbing. That was how her husband found her when he returned from work that evening.

The doctor paid them a house call and visited Lella in bed. He took her blood pressure, looked at her tongue, and felt her forehead. 'You must stay in bed,' he advised. 'It's time to take care of yourself now.'

Lella just closed her eyes and wished he would go away.

'Be gentle with her,' she heard him say in a lowered tone beyond the door. 'Her hormones are still unsettled and her body weak. She's been through a lot.' He prescribed some blue pills that would help her sleep, and instructed her husband not to allow her access to the news. 'I'm convinced it's this dreadful business that's brought on the anxiety, seeing all these parents lose their babies.'

Her husband had been given time off work, and he tended to Lella, bringing her cups of tea and boiled eggs that she didn't eat, and the blue pills with cool glasses of water. He watched her put each pill in her mouth and drink from the glass and then, satisfied, he would kiss her on the forehead and leave her to rest. She felt like a little girl.

When he was gone, she untucked the pills from beneath her tongue and slipped them over the headboard. She imagined them lined up on the carpet beneath the bed, gathering dust and fluff.

Lella also imagined the babies that she knew must still be disappearing. The ones she wasn't allowed to know about. Not knowing didn't help her own fear wane.

Her own baby she kept in bed with her at all times now, her arms close around her. It was the only way she felt safe. But with so little sleep her body seemed to be losing all its energy, and even lifting herself up against the pillows to feed the child was an effort.

Today, the baby was fractious. Her mouth strained as if she was hungry, but when Lella offered her the nipple she rejected it. Lella sang, and tried to rock her in her arms, but the baby wouldn't quieten. Eventually, Lella decided to try her in the cradle.

It was an effort just to pull back the covers, and when she did, despite the summer's day, Lella felt terribly cold in her thin nightgown. She held the baby against her chest and struggled over to the cradle where she laid her down carefully and tucked a blanket close around her. The baby was still crying, but as Lella rocked she eventually began to hush.

The rhythm of the rocking cradle made Lella's eyes begin to drop and her head loll. She kept jerking her eyes back open then struggling as desperately they tried again to close. The curtains were drawn against the day, and the only light in the room came from the bedside lamp. The baby was quiet now, lying calm beneath the blanket as the cradle rocked.

Once more Lella's eyes jerked open, and this time she let out a scream. A high, blood-curdling wail of a scream, for there at the foot of the cradle crouched a large grey rat. Its fur was greasy, and it had two long yellow front teeth biting beneath a shivering nose. Curled about its side and resting across the baby's feet was the thick pink sausage-meat tail. The rat's black eyes glittered in the light from the bedside lamp, fixed upon Lella.

On the table sat a cold boiled egg in an eggcup, beside four cold soldiers of toast. The butter knife rested on the edge of the plate. Snatching for it, she lifted it high to slash down at the rat, but at that same moment the door flew open.

'A rat!' she screamed, her eyes frantic and wide. 'Help me. There's a rat in the cradle! Look at it! There.'

Her husband grabbed for her wrist and as he clasped it tight the butter knife dropped from her hand. 'No!' she screamed, struggling backwards, her arm still raised above her head, 'Let go of me! I tell you, there's a rat. In the baby's cradle.'

'Lella,' he cried, trying to control her in his arms. 'Calm down. Stop it, stop it now. There's nothing. Look.' He forced her over so she could look. 'You see, nothing. You're fantasising, Lella. There's nothing there!'

She can't even scream. She can't yell. She can't do anything. Because he's right. All that lies on the tiny mattress is a neatly-folded blanket.

to hell with

SIMON ARMITAGE

THE CHRISTENING

I am a sperm whale. I carry up to 2.5 tonnes of an
oil-like fluid in my huge, coffin-shaped head. I have a
brain the size of a basketball, and on that basis alone
am entitled to my opinions. I am a sperm whale. When I
breathe in, the oil in my head cools to a dense wax and
I nosedive into the depths. My song, available on audio
cassette and compact disc, is a comfort to divorcees,
astrologists and those who have "pitched the quavering
canvas tent of their thoughts on the rim of the dark crater".
The oil in my head is of huge commercial value and has
been used by NASA, for even in the galactic emptiness
of deep space it does not freeze. I am attracted to the
policies of the Green Party *on paper* but once inside the
voting booth my hand is guided by an unseen force. Sometimes
I vomit large chunks of ambergris. My brother, Jeff, owns a
camping and outdoor clothing shop in the Lake District
and is a recreational user of cannabis. Customers who bought
books about me also bought *Do Whales Have Belly Buttons?*
by Melvin Berger and street maps of Cardiff. In many
ways I have *seen it all*. Jeff was actually christened
Geoffrey, but at his twenty-first birthday party declared
that no sexual partner can ever be truly satisfied by a man
whose name begins with the letter G. I keep no pets.
Lying motionless on the surface I am said to be "logging,"
and "lobtailing" when I turn and offer my great, slow
fluke to the horizon. Don't be taken in by the dolphins
and their winning smiles, they are the pick-pockets of
the ocean, the gypsy children of the open waters and
they are laughing all the way to Atlantis. Whale-watchers
unload their euphoria in great armfuls over the rails of their
catamarans and the gush of their sea-sickness is much
appreciated by birds and fish. On the basis of "finders-keepers"
I believe the Elgin Marbles should remain the property
of the British Crown. I am my own God – why shouldn't
I be? The first people to open me up thought my head
was full of sperm, but they were men and had lived
without women for many weeks and were far from home.
Stuff comes blurting out.

to hell with

DAREN KING

from MANUAL

The sky is pink
The clouds are blue
In Patsy's world
Everything is true

All around us were dogs. There were dogs talking and walking and flying. Dogs were howling round us in the wind. Dogs were lifting up. We had to keep from barking.

Patsy

I tell Patsy to keep away from the dogs. She looks confused, so I take her hand and lead her across the lawn.
    The grass is long, but dry. It has been a long, dry summer. The wind today is the arrival of autumn, blowing in from somewhere brown. Tomorrow, leaves will dance on the grass.
    "I'm sorry about the dogs. My son is coming to walk them. Don't worry, he won't come into the house."
    There's a stone birdbath here, which, according to Patsy, contains owl food.
    I ask Brandon what he does for a living.
    "I'm a doctor, a GP."
    This is the dining table, where Brandon eats his breakfast, reads *The Times*, opens the post.
    We sit and drink tea.
    Through the glass, we see the gate open, the son fasten leads round the dogs' necks.
    Patsy asks: "What sort of animal is that? They look like brown paper bags."
    This is Patsy's cowgirl outfit. Denim shirt, can-can dress. Black boots like old-fashioned kettles.
    "I thought you'd be dressed differently," Brandon says. "On your website you wear fetish gear."
    The website is an advert. It, I explain, is not real.
    Brandon tells Patsy how he likes to be beaten, the severity. He fetches a paddle, a gag, string. He likes to be tied into a chair and left.

Here, by the glass door.

I ask about the dogs, the son. He'll see you through the glass.

I instruct Brandon to strip to his underpants and stand, while Patsy and I make comments in rhyme. This is an idea Patsy had during the first session, and we've done it ever since. We focus on his hair, his physique. Your hair so fair, your back so slack. I bend him over the table, tie him to the tabletop. Here, by the glass door.

We sit on the patio and read *The Times*.

Mandar wants to meet in a café, to discuss. This is unusual. It will cost him extra. He is young, mid twenties. Mandar is sat at a table. Mandar looks at the coke can, the glass.

Patsy says he is an Indian prince. She wants to sniff his hair.

The waitress asks if we want anything.

Mandar hands me money. I stand by the table and count.

Patsy waits by the counter, arms folded behind her back, folded on the fake wood.

Mandar is bilingual, multilingual, and yet he cannot tell us what he wants.

"But what do *you* want?" Mandar asks us. "What would you do to me, if I said you could do anything you choose?"

What would we do?

Nothing. We would do nothing.

Patsy steps to the table, whispers in his ear. Mandar smiles, confused. Later, I ask Patsy what she told him. What did you tell him, what did you say?

She told him she once saw a homosexual cat.

Mandar moves his fingers on the coke, talks. "I'm getting married. I want to do something I have never done before."

Outside, clouds roll, gathering grey.

Mandar looks at the table.

The door opens, a line of glass sweeping the floor. Cars stop, start. A girl walks in, almond eyes, like Mandar's eyes.

The boy sits up, hand moves from the coke. He looks at me. His face tells me to walk away. She saw him from outside, was walking past, on her way somewhere, or home from somewhere, from work. Here is her boy, her fiancé, her Indian prince. Here, in this café, with this man, and the girl with boots made of tin.

"You said you wouldn't do it, Mandar."

"I'm not going to do it. I told him I don't want to do it."

In my hand, the money.

"You've paid him. Why pay him if you're not going to do it?"

Mandar and the girl walk out.

His hair, Patsy tells me, smelt of gunpowder.

"How about we massage each other, and we both get a happy ending?"

No. No happy ending.

We do not offer that service.

When we arrived, there was no Hugo. Only the red front door, the doorstep. Polite suburban terrace, Wimbledon. Trees shedding leaves, removing their clothes.

"Hi, I'm Hugo. How are you?"

This is how Hugo introduced himself. Not to Patsy, to me.

I waited with Patsy on the lawn. When I stepped onto the drive, my trainers were wet. Hugo's money will buy me a pair of winter boots.

Hugo fishes his key from his trouser pocket, his suit. His wife is at work, thinks he is at work. He was. He sneaked back.

Hugo tells us that the world of business is a series of levels, like in a computer game. Knowledge is accumulated.

Hugo is not understood. He can speak at a conference, he can delegate. He can command a sales fleet of forty. Yet, he cannot get through to his wife.

"I didn't realise there would be two of you. Did you bring oil?"

I did not bring oil, I do not offer that service.

Hugo has oil. His wife is a massage therapist. She works on his lumbago. This is the only time Hugo's wife is permitted to touch him. Her room is across the landing, the room they intended for their child, the child they will never have. But they will stay together, they took a vow. Hugo is a man of his word. A deal's a deal.

This, Hugo, is not a deal.

Hugo hides the plastic bottle in his hand.

"We travelled across London," I say in the bathroom. "You have to pay us, for our time."

Patsy hops across tiles, a game, do not step on the cracks.

We could tie him up, rob him, leave. But we cannot tie him up.

He does not want bondage. What Hugo wants is a full body rubdown. Patsy and Hugo have a conversation about self-defence. A trained nurse, Patsy knows how to protect herself.

Hugo twists to the floor, laughs, impressed. Patsy sits on Hugo, astride his chest, silk tie creased, a fold. "Stop now."

What if your wife comes home, Hugo?

Is this her photograph? Is this her face?

"My wife won't be back for hours. Stop now."

I tell Patsy that this is what he wants, that he is play acting, that he is a baby, what he really needs is a smack.

Patsy unbuckles Hugo's belt, awkward, tugs his pants down, lifts his legs, a mother changing a nappy, slap-slap-slap.

Hugo is not pleased. He does not want this. He wants it to stop.

"Sylvia won't be back for hours," Hugo says. "You can't sit on me all day."

I look at the clock.

Patsy bends Hugo's arm.

I walk down to the kitchen, count to ten, clang something, walk back up.

"What did you do in the kitchen?"

"I wrote a note for your wife."

I tell Patsy to help Hugo to his feet. He has something to find, on a different level.

On the stairs, Hugo unfolds his tie. Can you iron silk?

A car pulls into the drive.

"Where is it? Why are you doing this to me?"

"You have to give me the money."

Hugo hands me the money. I stand by the kitchen door, count.

"Where's the bloody note?"

There is no note. It is in your head. The car was a neighbour, turning round.

In the street, we look at the photographs.

Hugo, and his wife, Sylvia. Hugo and his empty home. His childless marriage, without love, without sex. The smell of massage oil. Bergamot, jasmine, lavender, rose. Patsy put the bottles into her bag.

Nathan hit a burglar with a frying pan. Hit him so hard the handle broke. The boy had climbed in the kitchen window. This window, by

Nathan's head.

"There's nothing like a biscuit," Nathan says, dunking the biscuit in his tea. "Do you want cash or cheque?"

Cash, in full, at the start.

Nathan chased the boy down the street. Knocked him off his mountain bike. Twenty years old. The pan span through the air, clonk.

Patsy ties Nathan to the radiator.

I open Nathan's piggy bank. Pull the pink plug. Coins fall out. It makes a lot of noise. 1p, 2p, 20p, 10p, 1p. On the shelf, on the floor.

Patsy tickles Nathan's belly with a feather.

I look in the fridge. Orange juice, from concentrate. Tin of corned beef, open, the metal lid curled, bent. Three cans of coke.

Nathan is bound, gagged. Nathan the fat, pink pig.

We use Nathan's duvet cover as a picnic blanket. This is unhygienic. What do you get up to in bed, Nathan? Do you keep the light on? Do you keep your socks on?

This is Nathan's list. Bondage, humiliation, verbal.

Nathan called the police as he ran. Yelled into his mobile phone. Held the boy in front of a CCTV camera till the police arrived.

We spread the tea things on the blanket. Corned beef sandwiches, the crusts cut off. Ice cream, jelly. Orange squash. On the cups, pictures of teddy bears at a picnic, like our picnic, though fun.

Patsy finds a bear in one of the children's rooms. A friend for Owl. Bear, you are coming home with us. Nathan doesn't love you anymore. Bear, meet Owl. Owl, meet Bear.

"Owl would turn his beak up," Patsy says. "Bears are working class. Bear has a PhD."

So Bear stays here, with Nathan.

Nathan is tied to the washing machine. Patsy ties Bear to Nathan's back.

In Nathan's study, a 5 megapixel camera.

Patsy finds a corkscrew in the cutlery drawer. A tail for the fat, pink pig. We do not proceed for legal reasons.

We smear jam on Nathan's bottom and take photos. Nathan has a study, a desk, a PC. Nathan has a photo printer. The PC gives us options. We print the photographs passport size, cut them out, hide them around the house. We do not know why we do this.

David lives above a pub in Tottenham. David sneaked us in round the back, up the back stairs.

David's wife is at work in the bar. David told us this.

This is David's lounge. The window, the wall unit, the television. The kitchen smells of brown sauce.

In the jar, flowers. Patsy picks through the flowers, stabs them into her hair. This while David eats.

I tell Patsy that she is a dancer, and she dances, nearly breaks the vase, the widescreen TV. Pirouettes, hurts her toes.

Do not tell Patsy things.

David closes the window, fastens the metal, swallows the last bit of sausage roll.

Explain it again, David.

"I want it to be like this dream I had, where Lorna came in and I'm tied up."

"Give her this." David hands me a note, the letters cut from newspaper. WE HAVE YOUR MAN.

We do not offer that service.

"Let me write on the back." David rummages, finds a pen, scrawls. It is a game. It is not real.

David takes off his jeans, shirt, socks. Flings his pants at a painting. Not a nice painting, and not nice pants. He lays on the bed, a pot-bellied star.

Your belly like jelly, your feet so neat.

Look at these CDs. What could be the soundtrack?

David has opera for lovers, the best of the sixties, the seventies, the eighties. Music to drive to, music to do the washing up.

"We need a sock," Patsy says, "for his mouth." She sorts through the drawer, finds a sock.

On the stairs, we listen. Music from David's plastic stereo, music from the bar.

In my hand, the note.

At the foot of the stairs, a door opens. "Who the hell are you?"

We're with David. Your husband. You live with. Upstairs.

"Upstairs? I live on my own."

Patsy kicks the front door.

If we leave, we will never know, never find out.

No, we should leave. This could get complicated. Angry

drinkers, regulars. Then, the police.

Not all emails are genuine. There are timewasters, hoaxers. There are people who do not know what they are doing. Many people are idiots.

A couple would like to hire our bedroom, our bed. Patsy thunders down the hall, to ask Owl.

Owl is not amused. Turns his head all the way round, in that way of his. Through the window, button eyes spy a vole.

Owl lives on that bed. The pillow is his nest, his home. A bird needs time alone. Owl needs a place to ponder. Owl is an intellectual, a thinker.

There are people making porn movies. They require someone to use, to abuse. Someone to hold the camera.

No, we do not offer that service.

We received an email from a journalist. I am writing an article on domination, fetish. Can we talk?

If you pay for my time, yes.

I met Tina in the Crown, a scruffy pub in Bethnal Green. Patsy waited in the wings, with Owl. Tina bought me a pint of London Pride. Her eyebrows were black, her fringe blonde. She asked questions, notebook open, pen poised.

What sort of people are your clients?

Well, what sort of people?

Are they all male?

I did not know, had nothing to say.

Patsy in her wooden chair at the back, rocking, lifting the legs. Owl sat atop the cigarette machine, watching pensively. Fell off when change clattered, rolled onto the floor.

"There is a lot I could tell you, Tina, but I am unable to do so for legal reasons."

What legal reasons? Michael?

"I am unable to discuss that for legal reasons."

Has something happened? Did a session get out of hand? Are you being taken to court?

"I am very anxious to clear my name."

In my hand, phrases cut from a newspaper.

Tina stood, walked out.

Patsy danced across the pub, pulled a man's belt loop, drank

Tina's drink. We brush dust from Owl's tummy feathers, laugh.

"Owl takes thins too seriously," Patsy says.

While Patsy is downstairs, clanging about, I do forty sit-ups. If I hear her clogs on the stairs, I will stop. I do not want to be laughed at, ever.

Owl turns away.

It is important, we are told. You have to look after yourself.

I look at the room. This is here, that is over there. If things move, I will know.

Patsy has packed two bags. One contains first aid, and Owl. One contains the plastic boxes. Patsy carries the bags. Patsy is strong, has the strength of the mad.

Outside, we step over flowers.

I ask Patsy why she brought a packed lunch, so much stuff.

"I think we will get kidnapped," Patsy says.

We walk to Bethnal Green tube. Central Line to Notting Hill Gate, Circle Line to Bayswater.

This is Thomas's Jag. This is the house.

Patsy puts the bags on the sofa, brown leather, creak.

Thomas has his head in his hands. Thomas stands from the armchair. Brown leather, creak.

Thomas's wife is dead. She was murdered, strangled. Died with fingers on her neck. "Her death has been the most terrible event of my life," Thomas says. "I cry very often uncontrollably."

On the table, a newspaper. The world of broadcasting becomes increasingly complicated to navigate, it says here. We turn away. We switch off.

Thomas tells us that she will never be. "She will never be." Never be what?

He sobs. Sobbing.

Thomas wants to be beaten. He wants to feel pain that is not mental, not emotional. Pain that is not inside.

Patsy removes Thomas's trousers, pants. Socks remain on. Red socks. Not the socks of a man in mourning, Patsy remarks. This whispered into my ear.

I tie Thomas to the coffee table.

Thomas stops crying. He is switched off.

Patsy smacks Thomas's bottom with the squash racket.

Thomas owns a permanent marker. It can write on anything, anything but itself. Remove the cap, write it down. We write words, phrases on Thomas's skin. Left, right, on his bum. I need my inhaler. My wife is dead.

Thomas will see these words, in mirror writing, in the bathroom. He will scrub them with salt.

I tell Patsy to untie Thomas.

"He will see the words," Patsy says, "reflected in Owl's shimmering gaze."

In Patsy's world, everything is true.

Thomas has an office, a study. He has a briefcase, a top drawer, an oak desk. Thomas has a cleaner. Monday, Thursday. Today is Thursday. The cleaner works at five, while Thomas is at squash. No squash today, Thomas.

We lie on Thomas's bed, hold hands. The cleaner will let herself in. She will find Thomas, scream, walk out. We will hear the key turn in the lock. This, from up here, in Thomas's bed.

We do not know what to do.

If we untie Thomas, he will hit us, become angry, shout. Or, he will weep.

We open the plastic boxes from Patsy's bag, eat the packed lunch. Sandwiches with the crusts cut off.

At ten to five, we let ourselves out.

Someone has been in our flat. Things have moved around. Not theft, everything is here.

The speakers, the sides that look like wood but are not wood, are here. The three circles that move, vibrate.

The television, not plugged in, no face.

Patsy, Owl, me.

Outside, shiny brown leaves sparkle, reflect the bright autumn sun.

Here is the bed, its squeak that Owl mistakes for a mouse, and swoops down to eat when Patsy throws him.

Here, the amp Patsy poured wine into. Her hands wide apart. Patsy thought her hands were close together. In one hand the bottle, the other, the empty wine glass. The hot machine sizzled. I switched off the mains, unscrewed screws, the magnetic screwdriver holding them. Beneath the lid, a city, the end of the world, the buildings futuristic, the rivers blood-red.

We dried the circuit board with tissue Patsy fetched from the bathroom.

Patsy is like me. She is someone who has experienced a lot of pain for no reason.

Here, Patsy's dressing up box, her wooden trunk. Inside, clothes mix together like paint. Not just clothes in there. Birthday cards, mirror, glitter. Anything that shines, excites.

At the window, trees dance in the breeze.

Patsy says it was Owl moved things. Flapped his wings and the room changed. Owl does not move things, I explain. Owl is inanimate, tired. Owl has beak flu.

Patsy fetches paracetamol, mashed up with cake.

I read the business news. The growing international crisis, catastrophic oil price spike, crude oil at over $100 a barrel. A single political shock could send the world market into panic.

"At lease we have our health," Patsy says. "Unlike poor Owl."

I tell Patsy it is not that simple. Analysts warn of a sharp rise in petrol prices. Empty forecourts, recession. If you can't afford petrol, you can't afford Patsy, me.

Patsy consults her owl book.

At the window, beyond the glass, trees hold hands.

Zero clients would mean zero income. No owl food or people food, no plastic bottles of supermarket wine. No home, no squeaky bed.

"Such business is not for owls," Patsy says. She covers his tufty ears. Cups the head with her palm. Owl does not need to hear this. Owl thinks we work in telecoms.

Beyond the glass, trees turn red.

Owl gets frightened easily. He needs a cuddle, every now and then, to make him feel safe.

Patsy sorts through her dressing up box, tossing clothes. Skirt over skirt, petticoat over skirts. Upside down, inside out. Her makeup is two black lines, one on each eye.

Through the window, office blocks, the windows clear as sea.

I show Patsy a photo of two dogs. The dogs look the same, are the same. The article explains that the dogs are sniffer dogs, trained to detect counterfeit DVDs. Their noses pick up the chemicals used in production. Piracy is linked to people trafficking, drugs.

Patsy says the dogs use their snouts.

Owl was knitted by an elderly lady. Patsy designed Owl herself, a flat shape on the back of an owl-coloured envelope, paid the lady two pounds, gave her day meaning.

Patsy has a self-destructive streak. I myself have a self-destructive streak. We are self-destructive. That is the worst thing to be because it means that you cannot become anything, that you will only ever be yourself.

Dogs have two hundred million sensitive cells in their nose, or snout. Dogs can taste smell, dogs do what they want. The dogs have not read the article. To dogs, the words have no meaning.

Through the window, office blocks glisten.

I have a feeling of pain. I am coming down with something. The feeling is in my muscles or joints. I can take paracetamol but that will take the pain away and then I will have nothing, only Patsy, who I love dearly, and also Owl.

The old lady knitted for two days, the wool dark as moss. She plumped him up, tried to give him shape. Stuffed him with white polyester cloud. Button eyes gave him meaning.

We arrived home last night to find the dressing up box moved. It had been by the window. On the bare boards, an oblong area without dust.

Owl could not have moved it. Owl is cushion-sized, plump.

Patsy can move the wooden trunk with one finger, one thumb. Patsy is strong as a pit pony, her description. But it wasn't Patsy who moved the wooden trunk. When I closed the door, Patsy was stood in the road.

Owl was here, and Owl is wise.

Who was it, Owl?

Did you see them? Did you catch them?

KEVIN CUMMINS

FLAGS

to hell with

PAUL FARLEY

CHALK: AN EPISTLE

I'm writing from a box bedroom of childhood,
breeze-blocked in one past life. If I wrote 'Rain
moving in from the west' or 'Irish Sea: good'
you'd catch my damp drift, could easily clone
the sea wall I slept next to, the escarpment
wind that rakes the landing, lifting up
the letterbox. Ideas become fitments
and before you know there is a northern landscape
and me inside a lit window within it,
cosily setting down this black wet idyll,
the whole thing up and running in a minute,
a second. Let me stop you in the middle:

I'm only interested in chalk. I've had enough
of what surrounds me. If this is to work
imagine how, today, I've pulled the legs off
creatures, spat and been spat on, got kicks
from setting fire to things, and in the cruel light
of my imagination and a bedside
lamp, I've opened up a book to write
myself out of the day, dusting its blackboards
down. So, clean and blank, I start again

using my library of Ladybirds.
I'm writing this for you in one of their flyleaves,
the only kid around here who believes
these full-colour illustrations of the South.
Bright red post vans climbing from village mists,
look-outs calculating the curve of the earth
from cliff-tops, spying as a clipper's masts
sail beyond the publisher's remit: *What to Look For in Spring*
means what grows in, or turns up on, British soil.
I've scoured the days and never found a thing
but read these books in bed and pray it's all
happening elsewhere. Did those illustrators
have any idea that they inspired
such devotions in the North? Am I a traitor
for harbouring such thoughts? Either way, I've wired
a landscape up: the picture-books have brought
the same faithful construction work to mind,
the sunken lanes dusty and white have caught
their corridors of day-heat; rivers wind

their way slowly to sea, rivers with names
from maps – Adur, Arun – which I can stock
and fringe carefully with other names which come
from the *Observer's* books. I know it like
the scaled down universe of the hobbyist
who walks giant-like between papier-mâché hills;
as intimately as a shower or sea mist
will feel its way inland. I dwell in details
and learn how words can be things in themselves:
these maps that haven't seen service outdoors
have place names stepping out beyond the shelve
of beaches, into the blue, like little piers,
and on the spoiler of a Brighton train
I hurl in sped-up footage for this coast,
from the clinker of Victoria, through the grain
of fifty miles of bramble, to the last
great buffers, with the sea at the end of the road,
where 'Brighton' is the word 'Britain' switched on,
every day is Whit Monday and I'm a Mod
being baton-charged along the shingle. Then

putting out the light, my fringed lampshade
leaves the afterimage of a jellyfish,
and I'm plunged into a warm sea without words,
and let the pre-historical saline wash
the wounds clean. After all this rushing about
my frame of reference is barely a film
a molecule-thick, picked up by slant sunlight.
The Chalk-hill blues flittering between Latin names
are doing so on an eternity's skin,
a mass, unnumbered burial at sea,
a steady marine snowfall; skeletons
of creatures off the end of a pin, algae
who had their lives to lead as we do now.
The surface scratched, the bone-pile underneath
revealed, you'd think might lead to nightmares, though
suspension in the fluids before Truth
and Faith and Valour is strangely comforting.

And so I'd wipe my slate and sink to sleep
each night by carefully imagining
a chalkscape. I see no reason to keep
to this story of me writing from a room
in childhood: over thirty million years
of mindless building work and one mad zoom

at the end, a couple of decades here and there
will make so little difference as to mean
sweet nothing. And I have lived on chalk for a year
at the end of the millennium: summer storms
stacked up over the Channel, the West Pier
still in its slow collapsing fade, great swarms
of birds like northern lights in negative
trawling for home, that bookshop's big window
with millions of closed pages on the move,
all intricate, unreadable, vast and slow.

   Sea floors, water levels, old horizons…
Is there some vestige of a memory
which made me feel nostalgic for the Downs
and Weald before I'd been there? Did I see,
beyond the bright green hills, the washed blue skies
of books, the solving undercoat of chalk
as paradise? This picture book disguise
which took me in had shallow seas like milk
beneath it, all the time, a nourishment
tapped into after rain-dark sandstone hours.
And whether this lies in my bones, or is heaven sent,
My mind, idle, at rest, always goes there.

LIAM McILVANNEY

IT STARTED WITH THE FLUTES

It started with the flutes. Thin, high, silvery – a sound that seemed too high for human ears, as if you'd acquired the hearing of a dog. The flutes were what carried furthest, not the drums, whose distant footfall kicked in shortly after. Up close, the drums were all you could hear, and the flute-players – eyes flashing irritably between visor and busy lips – might just as well have been miming. But in those first seconds the flutes held their own, and their wispy, weightless whispering was the loudest thing of all.

You heard it fitfully, at first, in gusts and snatches. There was a moment of uncertainty, a spell of anxious head-twisting when the music seemed to ring from all directions. Then some internal radar pointed down a canyon of vacant street and you ran, at a breathless gallop, to the oncoming clatter.

When the Walk turned the corner it pulled you up; you stopped short, winded by this glorious irruption. Youths in scarlet tunics and feathered caps swung onto Crosskirk High Street six abreast. Their buttons flashed. Their trouser-legs had stripes up the sides. Burnished flutes were pressed to their lips. They had the shallow perfection of figurines. Behind them came the walkers, in dark suits and clean shirt-collars, tasselled sashes, the women in churchy hats, some of them clutching bibles and umbrellas. Above them the banners pitched and swayed: dark likenesses of martyrs and reformers, the white smudge of King Billy's charger.

The onlookers whooped and clapped as the band approached, the air already pulsing with the drum. Out in front, drawing the roars of the crowd, came Jack the Lad, Cock of the Walk, the boy who swung the stick. He was talisman and witch doctor. All the fervour of the crowd, all their sense of favour and entitlement was focussed on his mobile frame. His specialness was there in all he did: in his rolling monkey-walk; how he crouched and sprang and strutted and twirled. You saw the beauty of it, his wayward figures-of-eight setting off the marchers' ordered tread, how their gait looked all the straighter for his flourishing arabesques. Grimacing, lolling, acting the goat: he might have been the town drunk were it not for the precision of his hands, the quick wrists busy with the stick. He stretched to send it spinning into the air and then stooped to let it roll across his shoulders or twirl in florid cartwheels round his back. I could watch forever the sluggish tinkle of his fingers as the baton rode the knuckles of one hand.

A girls' accordion band came next, teenagers in pleated kilts and crisp white fitted shirts, and the roaring was different now, lower and more throaty, and the girls lips twitched, as if with incipient laughter, their eyes sliding to take in the crowd.

I had an urge to cross, to step right out between the bands, make a break for the opposite pavement. You couldn't cross a Walk. You couldn't pass in front of it. We'd had this hammered into us as kids. The marshals would lift their truncheons in white-gloved hands and the polis would watch them strike you down.

I didn't cross. I watched the rest of the parade, the bands from Ayrshire and Ulster, the Toronto band with its maple leaf flag, marching down the low-roofed street, and when the last drummer banged past the Hall and the crowds moved off behind him, I followed too, down the hill to the Green.

Three days before this I was in Cox's office. Jenna, his PA, set a coffee down in front of me. On his desk, where the smirking offspring ought to have been, was the snap of Vinnie Jones reaching behind him to squeeze Paul Gascoigne's testicles. It was autographed in the bottom corner. Cox's windows faced west. He left me time to admire the downriver vista – the Armadillo, the Finnieston Crane – before emerging from his inner office.

Cox didn't rate me. I knew without him telling me that he thought my stuff was useless. Ponderous, he no doubt deemed it. Wordy, worthy, deficient in – let us say, bite? Malice? The note of personal enmity? Cox's own editorials had an unruffled viciousness that I enjoyed without wishing to emulate. Someone had told him I'd studied at Oxford and he was eager to let me know that he wasn't impressed. Why should he be? But I liked to wind him up. As the weeks passed, my copy grew pompously Latinate, I quoted from Bentham and Mill. I dug out my college tie when I knew we'd be meeting.

I was wearing it now as I told him the story. The story was Peter Lyons. I had a source who could connect him to loyalist paramilitaries in the early 1980s. I knew Cox would jump at this, so instead of talking it up, I found myself demurring: the details were sketchy; the source an unknown, most likely nursing a grievance. Probably it was horseshit.

Cox let me talk, his smile widening. He'd only been here two years, but he knew his readers. In this part of Scotland, sectarianism sold. It was better than sex. Then I showed him the photograph: Peter Lyons – or a man who looked like a younger version of Lyons – in a row of grinning men; the two figures in the foreground, sporting full-face balaclavas and pointing Webleys at the floor; and behind them on the wall, the claret-and-amber UVF flag.

Cox appraised it like a connoisseur. He got up from his seat, closed the connecting door to Jenna's office, and brought his chair to my side of the desk. There was a deliberation to Cox's movements. He never hurried. He seemed to relish the simplest physical action.

I liked his composure. It reassured me. If the office rumours were right, he had six months to turn the *Trib* around, two of which had already gone. We were bumping along at 55,000, same as when he took over. Every Tuesday, morning conference was a stampede of suggestions; ruses and stratagems for adding the four or five thousand that might save the title. The mood was hysterical. We were more like a self-help group than a conference of editors. Only Cox stayed calm, shirt-sleeved elbows on the table, setting out the week's agenda with slow chops of his big hands, smiling all around the anxious circle.

He was smiling now.

'The Boy Wonder', he said. 'Paramilitary of the Year.'

Two weeks ago, Lyons had won Parliamentarian of the Year at an awards dinner in the Copthorne Hotel. Cox and I had been sitting at his table. He bought us champagne to celebrate. We'd run a profile of him in that Sunday's paper.

'Who's the source?'

'That's what I'm saying, he's an unknown. There's no form.'

'What do you think?'

I turned up my hands.

'I think he's telling the truth.'

'OK. Let's find out. Have you spoken to any of the others, the old associates?'

I mentioned Gordon Orchardton, the New Covenanters. I told him about the Walk that coming Saturday, the big parade in Lyons's home town.

'Perfect', he said. 'Talk to the punters - get them oiled, sing the bloody Sash. See what turns up.'

I nodded. I ought to go to Belfast too, he said. Do some digging. He could send Martin Moir (he'd cubbed on the *News-Letter*, after all), but he'd rather I did it.

'I'll think about it.'

'Gerry.' I stopped at the door. He smiled up, back on his own side of the desk now. 'No old pals act this time, yeah?'

At my own desk I booted up and checked my emails. Cox thought the whole of Scotland was an old pals act, press corps and politicos deep in each other's pockets, so that only an Englishman – maybe only Norman Cox – could claim to be independent. He wasn't entirely wrong, but he wasn't right either. Peter Lyons wasn't a friend. I'd played Royal Troon with him a couple of times. His kids were the same age as the boys, and he'd brought them to our Paddy's Day softball game one year. And he was usually good for off-the-records. But he wasn't a friend, and that wasn't why I liked him. We all liked Peter Lyons. He was a good politician. He gave good copy. In a parliament of cloggers, he was Georgie Best. To hear some of his acolytes talk, he had saved the new Parliament from dying of embarrassment.

'A State is always disappointing,' wrote Denis Donoghue, 'especially one that has issued from a high rhetoric of race and nation. It is bound to incur the sardonic note of disillusion.' Lyons was elected to Holyrood in its second term, when the note of disillusion was deafening. Nobody had a good word to say about the Parliament. All the talent had stayed at Westminster. We had gone through three First Ministers in four years, each more mediocre than the last. The building itself was still a hole in the ground, into which was disappearing a torrent of public money. The MSPs themselves were a shambles. Spooked by the cameras, awkward in their stiff three-pieces and trouser-suits, they mumbled and stuttered through slapdash debates. Even our scandals were second-rate – stooshies over office rents and fiddled taxi claims.

Then Peter Lyons was elected on the Glasgow list. Nobody knew him. He hadn't been a councillor or Party researcher. He hadn't even been a member of the Party until the year before. Within six months he was Deputy Minister for Transport; a year later he was Justice Minister. By the following Spring, the scandal had broken. Someone unearthed a photograph of Lyons in the regalia of an Orangeman. He'd been a member of the Order in his teens and early twenties. He threw the stick in the Orange parades. A spokesman for the Catholic hierarchy expressed his sadness and alarm. The Record ran a mock-up of Lyons as William of Orange, astride his white charger. 'Can You Ride This Out, Peter?' was the strap line. Remarkably, he did. He went on Good Morning Scotland and spoke about his childhood. Since he'd been a kid, he said, he'd dreamed of being an Orange drum-major. In other parts of the country, the wee boy's dream was playing for Scotland; in Crosskirk it was throwing the stick on the Twelfth. Eventually he'd come to see that there were bigger ambitions, worthier dreams. He'd gone to university, his horizons had expanded. He'd come to see the Order for what it was, and he'd left. He wasn't a bigot. He had married a Catholic; his two kids were at Catholic school. The story became one of triumph over circumstance, the bright boy rising above the meanness of his origins.

Lyons had grown up in Lanarkshire, in an ex-mining village gone to seed, a sleet-stung bunker of cold grey stone. As Catholics, we mythologised these places, spoke of them with a shiver of dread. Harthill. Larkhall. Crosskirk. Even the names had a spondaic bluntness, a fearsome Prod foursquareness. You shook your head when you spoke them, made that noise you make when you've swallowed something burny. Now I was heading down the M74 on the morning of the Twelfth, peering through the smirr for the Crosskirk turn-off.

I'd never been to Lyons's home town. 'Bitter' was the term you'd hear. A bitter town. We had a kind of league table of bitterness, with all the shitty towns of Ayrshire and Lanarkshire graded by how much they hated Catholics.

The turn-off appeared, and I swung onto a B-road. The rain was clearing now, claustral shafts of sunlight falling on hedges and fields. Lanarkshire was shining in the rinsed air, nothing at all like the slagheap I'd envisioned. The road skirted a field, and through a break in the hedge I saw a hare skittering off down the furrows. I opened the sun-roof to birdsong and branches.

I thought about Mureton. On our bitterness league table, my home town wasn't high. No-one ever called me a Fenian bastard. I never felt menaced coming home from school. That doesn't mean we weren't keeping score. You knew how many Catholic bank managers there were in town, how many Catholic GPs, how many lawyers. The pub I drank in – the Star Inn (prop. J. Molloy) – was known as the Vatican. There were occasions when someone, hearing your surname, would narrow his eyes – 'Conway?'– and roll your name around his mouth, tasting something sour, and his silence would have the shape and weight of four unspoken words: *That's a Fenian name.*

St Michael's, Mureton's Catholic Church, stood on a hill beside the train station, in what had been a slum quarter. For decades it had been hidden from view by the great black façade of the town's Infirmary, but when the hospital was demolished and the chapel stood alone against the skyline, visible from almost everywhere in town, the town didn't like it. People complained about the old Infirmary, what a shame it was to see it go. What really riled them was the view it left behind, the papish chapel, *brazen* there, at the crown of the brae. Let them go to the devil in their own way, if that's what they wanted. Did they have to shove it down your throat?

But did I ever feel threatened or even put upon? You knew you were different, and when the St Michael's played away, and we took the field in our Milanese red-and-black stripes, there was an edge to some of the touchline shouts. All those urgings to get stuck in, get intae this shower; you wondered if this vehemence was matched at every fixture. But our sense of grievance was sedulously nurtured, stoked more by tribal memories of shipyard gangers and hiring fairs than by anything in our daily lives. Our ire was reserved for SPL referees and perceived acts of bias against Glasgow Celtic Football Club.

The sky had cleared. Up ahead some walkers turned to watch me approach. Three lassies – they had mounted the grass verge at the sound of the car, and now their skinny arms stuck into the road. A thin cheer rose as I slowed just beyond them. There was a bit of confabbing and then two climbed into the back as the other – the pretty one, evidently – slid in beside me.

'You going to the Walk, mister?'

'Yep.'

'Can you take us right into Crosskirk?'

'If you'll help me find it.'

'You've never been?'

They were relaxed now, proprietorial, leaning forward in their seats, pointing out the turnings. The smell of them – lemony, chemical – filled the car.

'You've never been to the Walk?'

'Not this one.'

'It's major, man. There's bands from Ireland, all over. Canada. The Walk goes on for ever.'

'Scooby,' said the one right behind me. 'Nice ride. Is it turbo, mister?'

'Afraid not.'

'Hey, he looks like a pimp now,' said the one beside me. 'We're his bitches. D'you feel like a pimp, man?'

'Not especially.'

'You're mental, Diane.'

'What's your name?'

'Gerry.'

'Gerry!' They mugged disbelief. '*Gerry*? You a pape?'

'I'm a journalist.'

I slowed for an oncoming lorry.

'Are you writing it up for the paper; the Walk?'

'That's the idea.'

'Will you put us in?'

'What paper is it?'

'Where's your photographer?' Diane struck a pole-dance pose, hands above her head.

'It's the *Tribune on Sunday*. I don't have one.'

'Too bad.' She pulled the visor down, checked herself in the mirror, rubbed a finger along her teeth.

'Hey, you got anything to drink?'

'There's some water.' I nodded towards the glove compartment. 'In there.'

'He's looking at your legs, Diane.'

'Dirty bugger.'

She paused with the bottle in her hand.

'Are you looking at my legs?'

'No, I – '

'How no?'

The three of them sputtered, the two in the back leaning together till their heads touched. I looked around at Diane again. The set of her lips, or the line of her nose: something was familiar. I seemed to know her. Before I could place it we had reached Crosskirk, its long main street of brown sandstone.

'Can you drop us at the puggies?'

At the amusements arcade they climbed out and were swallowed up in the dark and noise and coloured lights. Two boys in Rangers tops by the door turned to check out their arses then glared back at me. Diane spun round, once, a cute 360 turn: a flash of teeth, a quick twist of the wrist, a ripple of white pleated skirt.

I drove up the High Street, past Boots the Chemist, the Masonic Lodge, Blockbuster Video, the British Legion. A stylised eye on a billboard advertised the current series of Big Brother. I passed a mural, stiff-limbed figures in balaclavas and black combat jackets, hardware held aloft: 'UFF 2nd BATT C COMPANY'. A knot of boys at the war memorial turned to watch me pass. Old fears began to surface. How Catholic did you look? Could people tell? Was the Forester's dark bottle green green enough to arouse suspicion?

Near the top of the hill, tied to a lamp-post was a cardboard sign with an arrow, a capital P and the logo of an Orangeman (bowler hat and chevron-shaped sash). I followed the arrow to a big stretch of wasteground in what looked to have been an industrial estate. It was busy already: buses and cars parked in makeshift lines. I left the Forester beside a Parks of Hamilton coach and headed out to see the fun.

I like the Walk. I know you're not supposed to. I know it's a throwback, a discharge of hate, a line of orange pus clogging the streets of central Scotland. But I like it anyway. I like the cheap music, its belligerent jauntiness. I like the crisp gunfire of the snares. I like the band uniforms and the hats and the apocalyptic names stencilled on the Lambeg drums: Cragside Truth Defenders; Denfield Martrys Memorial Band; Pride of Glengarnock Fifes and

Drums.

For most folk, a parade's an excuse to throw off restraint. In most parades, the participants take their cue from the bands, you think of Rio, its swirl of sequins and ostrich feathers, the bobbing phalanxes of militant Sowetans, Pamplona's neckerchiefed *riau-riau* dancers. And then there's Scotland's Orangemen. Here they come, in their Sunday suits, dark, with just that grudging flash of colour at the shoulders, step by dispassionate step, bibles closed, umbrellas rolled. Lenten faces and tight, teetotal lips. It's a carnival of restraint, a flaunting of continence. The music rolls past, sends out its invitation to swagger and reel. But the marchers step carefully on, unmoved, without the least roll of the hips.

All except for the drum-major, who dances enough for everyone. He takes up the shortfall, whirling and spinning, knocking himself out. All their sinful urges, all the demons of the tribe: he takes them into himself and dances them out. He's the leader, but there's something sacrificial too, like he's some kind of outcast or scapegoat. He's a mock monarch, the King of the Wood, raising a bandaged fist to pluck his sceptre from the skies.

On the sidelines, parts of the crowd catch the infection. They surrender to the music, cavorting on the pavement, drunkenly Stripping the Willow. But after all, these are only spectators, and the Order, in its official pronouncements, likes to stress its disapproval of hangers-on. Is this what bothers the high-ups, I wonder? Not the drunkenness and the battle songs, the tally of cautions for breach of the peace. Just the sheer enjoyment, the looks on the faces? The music plays and people dance.

When the march was over we went to the Green – a stretch of parkland down by the river. The speeches had already started: a small man in a tight suit was talking sternly into a microphone on a platform draped with Union flags. Those nearest him nodded and clapped. You knew when to clap because he left a space. The Green looked like an encampment. The bandsmen had laid down their drums and flutes and were cracking open cans and bottles. The smell of fried onions carried from the food vans. Bannerettes were laid out on the grass, side by side, like the frames of a comic strip. Two toddlers in kilts were sword-fighting with flutes. A man strolled between the groups, handing out little booklets. 'Have You Met Your Redeemer?' I stuck it in my back pocket. Three guys sitting on a Union flag were playing pontoons for matchsticks.

At the far end of the meadow a kick-about was underway on the flat ground by the river: a fat man rushed to keep the ball out of the water and landed on his arse once he'd hooked it clear. His raised arm acknowledged his comrades' cheers.

People had brought flasks and tartan rugs, jumbo bottles of cider and fizzy juice, towers of plastic cups.

I passed a family of five enjoying a full-scale picnic. The father had the cool-box open and was twisting a can of lager from its plastic loop when my shadow fell across him. He looked up, nodded hello, and held out the can; gave a no-worries shrug when I shook my head.

I kept an eye out for Diane, but the field was thronged. Teenagers were necking behind the burger vans. A boy with stringy hair was puking into the river. I picked my way back through the fallen bodies. It was hot and sticky. I thought of the can of cold beer and wished I'd taken it.

At the Cross Keys Inn, a solitary barman skidded back and forth behind the counter, stretching to press the optics, squatting to snatch beer bottles from crates. He kept at least three taps in motion, flicking each one just before it overflowed. In between he plucked banknotes from fists and dropped change into palms. Compared to the barman the drinkers looked static. Jammed in tight, they could barely move. They turned their heads fractionally to slurp from pints or tear bites out of filled rolls. Up close, there was something camp about the bandsmen. It was the uniforms, the military cut twinned with toyshop colours – superhero reds and blues. They looked like pantomime soldiers, their jackets loud with piping, gold braid criss-crossing the chests, running in garrulous spirals round the cuffs.

Filled rolls wrapped in cellophane were piled on the counter. Spilled beer formed muddy slicks on the brick-coloured lino. The smell was high: top notes of sweat and flatulence over the radical pub stink of slops and stale baccy, pish, disinfectant. I fought my way to the bar and held out a tenner. Ten minutes later, Mary Slessor still in hand, I needed to piss. I pushed back to the exit and joined the row of marchers lining the back wall. By the time I made it back, the place was starting to empty. Pints and whiskies were swilled and sunk and the bandsmen moved out, fastening collars and cuffs, pulling Glengarrys from their epaulettes.

'Where's the fire?' I asked my neighbour.

'It's the return leg: they march back up to the kirk.'

'You not marching yourself?'

'No me.' He added water to his whisky. 'My job's done.'

'How's that?'

'I'm a marshal, son. We bow out at this point, and they're glad to see the back of us. Let the boys cut loose a bit. Do the blood-and-thunder stuff.'

He seemed to think of something.

'What's yours, anyway?'

He added my order to his own and the barman shouted, 'Got it.' He was rushing around as if the bar was still busy, though only the regulars were left – a few pensioners nursing tumblers of Bells, ponies of seventy shilling.

'There you go, son.'

'Good man.'

'Frazer Macklin.'

I shook his hand.

'John.'

'Okay John. You coming over?'

I helped him carry the drinks.

We joined the others, three men in dark suits at a corner table. They seemed unsurprised at my arrival, jerked their chins in tepid greeting as if I drank here every day. They had the bored, competent air of petty officials – ticket inspectors or shop stewards. Their sashes and white gloves were folded in two neat piles on the windowsill behind them. Without their regalia they seemed closer to the elderly regulars than to the departed bandsmen. They didn't have much to say. One of them told an anecdote about his grandson and a pet shop. There was a half-hearted colloquy about Rangers' latest transfer target.

The man sitting across from me wore white training shoes. He saw me notice.

'I've got bad feet,' he said. 'The Walk's a killer.'

I got a round in. They all drank heavy, except for one who was on Black-and-Tan. He looked at me queerly when I set it in front of him.

'Is that not right?'

'What? No, it's fine, son. Spot on.'

The barman aimed the remote and the racing came on, a close up of galloping fetlocks swathed in white tape, then a long shot of the field.

The Black-and-Tan man was staring: I could feel his gaze on the side of my face. Finally he leaned forward.

'Do I know you, son? Are you a Brother?'

I'd already clocked the signet ring, the compasses and square.

'Naw.'

'Do you work in IBM?'

'I don't, no.'

'I've seen your face.' He shook his head. 'It'll come to me.'

Frazer went out for a smoke and when he came back we were still discussing the smoking ban. For the first time since I'd joined them, the Orangemen were animated. They came alive in the clamour to badmouth their new politicians, to bemoan the peerless nullity of the Parliament. The smoking ban was the least of it. An infringement of civil liberties, said one of them. The thin end of the wedge. They spoke about creeping totalitarianism, the need for constant vigilance.

'That's right. One day you cannae spark up a Regal; the next it's popery and wooden shoes.'

'That's no funny, son.'

Everyone slags the Parliament: it's a staple of bus-stop small-talk, like the weather or the state of Scottish football. But the Orangemen had their own slant, their own angle of grievance.

'Have you seen the names?' said the man with the training shoes. 'Fucking Kellys and Connollys and Maguires and fuck knows what. Scottish Labour Party? Scottish Sinn Fein.'

'Behave yourself, Turner.'

'Home Rule is Rome Rule. We said it all along, and guess what? It's true.'

'Yeah, but they're no all like that,' I said.

Turner shrugged.

'This was Lyons's lodge, wasn't it?'

'What's that, son?'

'Peter Lyons.'

Nobody spoke. Finally Frazer peered into his half-pint glass, swirling an inch of seventy.

'It's a long time since Peter Lyons threw a stick.'

'But did you know him then? What was he like? Was he a good Orangeman?'

'Of course I knew him. He was a bloody good drum major, that's what he was.'

The others nodded.

'The best', said Turner.

'So what happened?' I looked round the faces. 'Why did he leave?'

'He sold the jerseys,' said Black-and-Tan. 'He wanted his name on election posters. He wanted a red rosette and his picture in the papers. He knew the comrades wouldnae wear it, the selection committees, what have you.'

'Yeah, but you never really lose it, do you?' Frazer tapped on the tabletop. 'He'll always be an Orangeman.'

'Don't kid yourself, Brother.'

'I'm not kidding. I'll tell you one thing. I remember his face when he led the band, the look in his eyes when he brought the boys down that High Street. I don't care what he does, I don't care he becomes Prime Minister, the bloody Pope, he'll never get a feeling the like of that.'

'Do you never see him any more,' I said. 'Does he never come down, for the Twelfth?'

Frazer set the empty glass on the table.

'Why'nt you ask him.' He nodded at an old boy sitting at the bar. 'That's his faither.'

We all looked across. The old man rose to his feet and edged out from behind his table. I thought at first he had heard us and was leaving, but he walked past the exit, heading for the lavatory. Then the barman had his arm out, pointing across the pub:

'That'll do you, girls. Not another step.'

Three lassies, in short skirts and heavy eye make-up, stood just inside the door. Diane was the leader. She held up a card, brandished it like a referee.

'What's this look like? You cannae bar us mister. We're eighteen. We've got ID.'

'It's your bus pass, hen. You're no coming in.'

He was out from behind the bar now, approaching with outstretched arms, shooing them out.

Diane looked around.

'Hey Gerry! There's Gerry. Tell him, Gerry. We're eighteen. Tell him.'

'Out.'

The door swung shut on their protests. The barman stayed where he was, making no move to go back to the bar.

Black-and-Tan was nodding. He reached for his drink and then stopped.

'You're Gerry Conway. I fucking knew I knew you.'

'Who's Gerry Conway?'

'He writes for the *Trib*. You write for the *Tribune*.'

'You're a journalist?'

I nodded.

The man who was Peter Lyons's dad had come back from the toilet now and he too stopped, waited for what would happen.

There was a long, slack moment of silence, during which I studied the scuffs on the lino and Turner's incongruous training shoes, and then the breeze was cool on my face, lifting my fringe.

The barman was holding the door.

'Time you werenae here, son.'

I couldn't find the car. I walked from one end of the waste-ground to the other. More than ever, it looked like a football match; all the buses in a row, Rangers placards in their windows: Garscube Loyal; Tradeston True Blues. Then I turned a corner and there it was.

The parade had finished: the pavements were filling up once more, as bandsmen and marchers went back to their coaches. I inched through the streets, stop-starting, gently beeping the pedestrians. I wanted out before the streets clogged altogether, and I turned, without proper attention, onto the High Street. I clocked it straight off: the blue disk, the white arrow, pointing the wrong way. Shit. I looked for a side-street, but they were thick with bodies, the crowds spilling into the thoroughfare. Fuck. I threw the car into reverse and swung round.

At first I thought I'd hit someone: shouts of protest sounded from the rear. Something banged on the roof. A hand appeared beside me making the 'wanker' gesture – no; he wanted me to roll down the window. No chance: I shook my head. He jabbed his finger at me, then at the 'One Way Street' sign. *I know*; I nodded. The crowd was thick on either side now, the car stuck sideways across the white line.

Two middle-aged guys stepped round the bonnet, and one of them paused: the Cross Keys guy, the Black-and-Tan drinker. He grabbed the other's sleeve and pointed. The second man turned, gestured to someone behind him.

I leaned on the horn; the sound was thin and somehow effete. It brought more onlookers round the car. I revved the engine but nobody moved. Black-and-Tan stayed out in front with his palms on the bonnet, as if waiting to be frisked. His eyes were dull with drink.

Pointlessly, as if a winking yellow light would bring everyone to their senses, I applied the left indicator.

A gob splattered the windscreen. Someone was trying the door. There was an icy tinkle, barely audible, that I knew was a headlight breaking.

My bag was on the passenger seat: I scrabbled in the side pocket, fingers paddling for my phone. More spit slid down the glass. The banging on the roof started up once again. I saw a man lean backwards to give himself room, and a shoe-sole the size of a suitcase came pistoning towards me.

I found the phone.

As I thumbed the buttons a different noise cut through the hubbub, a thin slicing sound, hissing at the window. I craned round. For a moment the whole scene – the jostling bodies, the opening mouths – had a barley-sugar tinge, an orangey film, and I was back in my childhood sick-bed, viewing the world through the cellophane wrapper of a Lucozade bottle. Then the window cleared and a brown cock jiggled comically for a second before flipping into a waistband.

The cabin darkened: someone was up there, blocking the sun-roof. Then he was down again and my ear was hurt, stinging, as if something has struck it. My bag thudded down from the passenger

seat and the mobile jumped out of my hand. The glove compartment slumped open and my CDs skittered out. Through the front
windscreen the sun was swinging into my eyes and out again, like a
torch clicking on and off.

They were rocking the car.

Three or four bodies on either side, working together, hitting a
rhythm. Each time the car rocked to the right, the window thumped
into my ear. I braced my right arm on the door-frame and gripped
the handbrake with my left. The windscreen kept pitching like a
boat on heavy seas, a little steeper with each new heave. Then the
sun flared in my side window, not the front, and I was rising,
floating, suspended in air as the car tipped onto its fulcrum.

Even then, as a rhombus of blue sky paused in the window, and a
vast protracted second gave me all the time in the world to review
my situation, I didn't feel afraid. That I might be seriously hurt, in a
small town in Lanarkshire, on a sunny weekend afternoon, by a
crowd of militant Calvinists in blue suits and sashes, seemed – even
then – unrealistic. How serious were these people? How angry? I
don't think they themselves were sure. Had something happened,
had the car tipped over and the windows shattered, with shards and
splinters and blood on the roadway, they might have claimed it as a
joke, a prank, a piece of wayward fun. And they might have been
right. At that point things could have gone either way.

Then the chassis was bouncing with the shock of impact and ironic
cheers greeted my landing.

I waited for the rocking to start again but the bodies had moved
away, the cabin suddenly bright, and a policeman's face –
incredulous, angry – loomed at my elbow. He rapped on the window.

Out front another cop – arms spread wide in a green fluorescent
jacket – was moving back the crowd. A blue light whirled mutely
from a squad-car.

I pressed the button.

'Are you alright?'

'Yes.'

'Jesus Christ.' He glanced round the cabin as if hoping to spot
whatever had riled the crowd. 'Right. Let's get you out of this. Stick
close to us. Alright? We'll take you the Uddingston road.'

The window scrolled up.

I put the car in gear and eased round. The squad car pulled off. The crowd closed behind me, raising its noise.

On the motorway, once the cops had taken the exit and I merged back into the citybound flow, I still felt shaken. The backs of my arms prickled with shame. The rocking of the car hadn't bothered me. It was the slow drive down Crosskirk High Street, the hard laughter of the crowd. The street had seemed to go on forever. At one point, when the cop-car braked without warning, I stalled. The crowd hooted and cheered. I saw the camera phones, the hands cupped around shouting mouths. For a second I was lost, I no longer knew how to drive a car. Then I closed my eyes and opened them, talked myself through it: turn the key; find first gear. I followed the Range Rover's bumper down that hostile mile, beneath loops of coloured bunting. It felt like an expulsion, the town purging my unclean presence. I wasn't the victim but the culprit, the scapegoat, the treacherous Lundy.

The faces stayed with me, on the drive back to Glasgow, and the smirking grins on Crosskirk High Street meshed with those in the photo of Lyons. These were Lyons's people, this was his hinterland. This is where he preened and swaggered, tossing his stupid stick. Suddenly I was rooting in my pocket, yanking out my phone. I stopped in a lay-by and punched the number.

'Norman Cox.'

'I'll need a week,' I told him. 'I'm going to Belfast.'

DALJIT NAGRA

X

                    i knot my tongue
i nail my lips
i zip my lids

            & still u say
            i say   u harm

u hook my arms
u hood my head
u lose my legs

            & still u say
            i say   u harm

KARELA!
(for Katherine)

Gourd, grenade-shaped,
okra-green. I prise
each limb of warty flesh,
disembowel each indi-
gestible red-seed memory
of regal pomegranate.
This dish from my past, I recall
mum would embalm the innards
with amalgam of fried onion
to gum the snarled temper.
Mummy-bound with string
for a mustard popping pan.
Then sealed. Masala creeps...

Karela, ancient as crocodile,
no matter I kiln-crisp
each skin for ages, proudly
before my English lover,
when the lid comes off
each riven body shrivelled
yet knurl-fisted and gnarled,
blackening centuries of heat
with a feedback of sizzling
smoke and wog – rescinders
stoking my mind with inedible
historical fry-ups. The rebel
ethic of our ethnic gumbo!

Hail to the King of Bile
as I bite a mean mouthful
swamping me down to the tracts
of my roots – my body craves
taste of home but is scolded
by shame of blood-desertion
(that simmers in me unspoken),
save that we are in love –
that you bite as well your mind
with karela-curses, requited
knowledge before our seed
can truly bloom, before
our tongue is pure poppy!

to hell with

BENJAMIN MARKOVITS

JOURNAL WEST

1

God Discusses West Texas

At first there's nothing.
I want to teach patience.
The trick is, not waiting.
I give them repetitions:
low bushes, telephone poles,
shacks, cars.
Also, lines:
roads, telephone wires.
In other words, directions.
It's very flat.
There's nothing to wait for.
Then something happens.

A hill.

2

New Mexico

I think mainly about colour.
I have so much space,
especially here.
I chose red hills
for New Mexico.
A girl on a lucky day
dresses brightly.
She doesn't care who looks.

Next I consider shapes.
Clouds, for instance.
They are much like me –
flexible.
I play with them for ages.

I saw a street sign:
HENRY'S IRRIGATION & MACHINES
FULL PUMP-SERVICE.
I leave them the detials.

3

Kadish

A Kiwi
in a big hat
with a sun-burnt face
and a big moustache
knocked off six bucks
from a spirit-lantern
for two young men
who otherwise
would not have bought it
outside Yosemite
last gas for fifteen miles.
He did so
because they asked him
where he came from
what his wife did.
She was dead.

The two young men
played cards
in a campground
outside Yosemite
beside the smoky lamp
which burnt
till eleven.

4

Yosemite

At the green sign
for VISTA POINT
the air across
Yosemite Valley
smells like artichoke.
There's a grape sun
setting over thin hills.
Below, lie or stand
lines of trees
leafless, with burnt arms,
leaning across
or straight in the back
as soldiers, rows
of bright dead trees.
Quiet as ash
after hell-fire.
My favourite grey
needs only
a withering look.

5

Butte, Montana

The hills shoulder
their way like whales
around Butte, Montana.
The town lies in the flat.
The wide streets, by brick
warehouses and pool halls,
are mostly empty.
Five years ago they built
a statue called
The Lady of the Rockies
in Butte, Montana.
They hauled her up
and stood her
on a shoulder of the hills.
Tourists come
to take a bus
to see the statue
on the hills
where they look down
on Butte, Montana.

6

Sabbath

I finished
after great labour
Wyoming.
My fancy, strange
and grand, poked
spouts in white land
that ran red.
I carved
of rarest mountain
and finest lake
the Grand Tetons.
Thousands came to look.

I went south
spent
to a big land.
I had no ideas.
From east to west
the ground lay
yellow and green.
There was too much space.

They put cows,
towns there,
and a very straight road.
I sat confounded
in Hugo, Colorado
and slept
and dreamt of nothing.

JON SAVAGE

INTERVIEW WITH KURT COBAIN

This interview was conducted around midnight in a midtown Manhattan hotel in July 1993, to promote Nirvana's then forthcoming album, "In Utero".
At that time the pre-release cassettes of the record included I Hate Myself
and I Want To Die, *a song that for me encapsulates Cobain's passion and his sardonic humour. Apart from some specific references to then recent events which are explained, I'm happy to let the dialogue stand. It's probably the last major rock interview I will ever do and it remains a powerful memory. JS*

I was born in Aberdeen, Washington, 1967, and I lived between Aberdeen and Montesano which was twenty miles away, and I moved back and forth between relatives' houses throughout my whole childhood...
Did your parents split up when you were young?
  Yeah, when I was seven.
Do you remember anything about that?
  I remember feeling ashamed, for some reason. I was ashamed of my parents... I couldn't face some of my friends at school anymore, because I desperately wanted to have the classic, you know, typical family. Mother, father. I wanted that security, so I resented my parents for quite a few years, cos of that.
Have you made it up with them now?
  Well, I've always kept a relationship with my mom, because she's always been the more affectionate one. I haven't talked to my father in about ten years now up until this last year, where he sought me out backstage at a show we played in Seattle. For a long time, I... I always wanted him to know that I don't hate him anymore, I just don't have anything to say to him.
I don't want to have a relationship with someone just because they're my blood relative. They bore me. My father is incapable of showing much affection, or even of carrying on a conversation, so... just because of the last time that I saw him, I expressed this to him and made it really clear to him that I just didn't want anything to do with him anymore. But it was a relief on both our parts, you know? Because for some years he felt that I really hated his guts...
That's really serious stuff. It really fucks you up, but you can't duck it.
  It's what I've done all my life, though. I've always quit jobs without telling the employer that I'm quitting, I just wouldn't show

up one day.

Same with high school, the last two months of high school, I quit, so I've always copped out of things, so to face up to my father was... although he chose to seek me out, you know? But it was a nice relief.

Do you write about this at all? There's a lyric on 'Serve the Servants'...

Yeah. It's the first time I've ever really dealt with parental issues. I've hardly ever written anything obviously personal, to myself or to anyone else, on that scale. I'm obviously alerted to that whole subject anyway...

When you were growing up, were you very isolated?

Yeah, very. Well, I had a really good childhood, until the divorce, then all of a sudden my whole world changed. I became antisocial, and... I started to understand the reality of my surroundings, which didn't have a lot to offer. It was such a small town, and I couldn't find any friends that I was very fond of, or who were compatible with me, with the things that I liked to do. I liked to do artistic things, and I liked to listen to music.

What did you listen to then?

Whatever I could get a hold of. My aunts would give me Beatles records, so for the most part it was just Beatles records, and every once in a while if I was lucky I might be able to buy a single...

Did you like the Beatles?

Oh yeah. My mother always tried to keep a little bit of English culture in our family, like we'd drink tea all the time! Although I'd never really known about my ancestors, until this year, that the name Cobain was Irish.

My parents had never bothered to look, to find that stuff out. I found out through looking through the phone books throughout America, for names that were similar to mine. I couldn't find any Cobains at all, I started calling Coburns, and I found this one lady in San Francisco who had been researching our family history for years...

So it was Coburn?

Actually it was Cobain, but the Coburns screwed it up when they came over. They came from County Cork, which is a really weird coincidence, because when we toured Ireland, we played in Cork and the entire day I walked around in a daze. I'd never felt more spiritual in my life. It was the weirdest feeling, and I have one friend who was with me who could testify to this, I was almost in tears the whole day. Since that tour, which was about two years ago, I've had like a sense that I was from Ireland.

What was your mother's maiden name?

Friedenberg, which is German. I think they pronounce it Frowdenberg.

Were they first generation?

I don't know. I only found out some of the information on the Cobain side, so far. I've never discussed ancestry with my mother. I still don't know a lot about the Cobains, the lady who I contacted is sending me some information. I haven't received it yet.

Were people unpleasant to you in high school? Did you kind of withdraw?

I was a scapegoat, but not in the sense that people would pick on me all the time. People wouldn't pick on me or beat me up, because I was so withdrawn by that time, and I was so antisocial that I was almost insane. I felt so different and so crazy that people just left me alone. I felt that they would vote me "Most Likely to Kill Everyone at a high school dance"...

Could you understand why people would do that? Or how people could get to that stage?

Yeah, I could definitely see how a person's mental state could deteriorate to the point where they would do that. Yeah. I've gotten to the point where I've fantasised about it, but I always would have opted for killing myself first. You know? I love movies about that. I've always loved revenge movies at high school dances and stuff like that. Carrie...!

There's an emptiness here that you don't get in England... in England you do feel connected to everyone around you, in a funny kind of way. You do feel as though, yes, you are recognisably on the same planet. Unless you are in a really alienated state. To me there is a huge hole in this country that comes from the eradication of the Indians...

Where I grew up there are about three Indian reservations. It's so depressing to go there. Right on the ocean, there would be... I think there was a time in the early 60s when the government decided to pay back the Indians in a way by up-scaling the reservations, and giving them appliances and stuff like that. They didn't want to deal with stuff like that, you'd go to the reservation and you'd see washers and dryers out in the front yard. They wanted their culture back, they didn't want washers and dryers.

And they're all fucked up on alcohol, which is the main killer of the whole race. Indians were considered the same as black people in the South, when I grew up, and it was their land. There weren't many Indians that even went to the public schools in my town, and its such a small place, they were even more isolated. They were looked down upon...

When did you first hear punk rock?
Probably '84. I keep trying to get this story right chronologically, and I just can't. I remember I found the Clash's 'Sandinista' at the library, and Ihated it. I thought, if this is what punk rock is, then I don't want anything to do with it. It's too bad, because I'd wanted to hear punk rock forever. Ever since Creem (US rock magazine: now defunct) started covering the Sex Pistols' last tour. I would read about them and just fantasise about how amazing it would be to hear this music, and to be a part of it. I was like eleven years old, and I couldn't possibly have followed them on the tour. The thought of just going to Seattle was just impossible. It was two hundred miles away. My parents took me to Seattle probably three times in my life, from what I can remember, and that was always on a family trip. I was always trying to find punk rock, but of course they didn't have it in our record shop in Aberdeen, then Buzz Osbourne... actually I probably bought Devo and Oingo Boingo and stuff like that, that finally leaked into Aberdeen many years after the fact. Then finally Buzz Osbourne (from The Melvins) in 1984 who'd been a friend of mine off and on between Montesano and Aberdeen, cos I'd moved so much, he lived in Montesano the whole time, he made me a couple of compilation tapes. Black Flag and Flipper, everything, all the most popular punk rock bands, and I was completely blown away. I finally found my calling. That very same day, I cut my hair and I would lip-sync to those tapes, I'd play them every day, it was the greatest thing. I'd already been playing guitar by then for a couple of years, and I was trying to play my own style of punk rock, what I thought it would be. I knew it was fast, and had a lot of distortion...
There were so many things going on at once... it expressed the way I felt socially and politically... it was the anger that I felt, the alienation. For so many years I couldn't understand why... although I listened to Aerosmith and Led Zeppelin, and I really did enjoy and still do enjoy some of the melodies they'd written, they were definitely lacking something, and it took me so many years to realise

that a lot of it had to do with sexism, the way that they just wrote about their dicks, having sex. That stuff bored me...

When did you start thinking about all that? It's very unusual for people in rock bands to think about that... did that come from punk?

No, it was before that. Because I couldn't ever find any good male friends, I ended up hanging out with the girls a lot, and I just felt that they weren't treated equally, weren't treated with respect, the way Aberdeen treated women in general. They were just totally oppressed, the words bitch and cunt would be totally common, you'd hear it all the time. But it took me many years after the fact to realise those were the things that were bothering me. I was just starting to understand what was pissing me off so much, and within that year, the last couple of years of high school, and punk rock. It all came together, I finally admitted to myself: I am not retarded, you know?

Did you have problems with people thinking you were gay?

Yeah. I even thought that I was gay. I thought that might be the solution to my problem. One time during my school years, although I never experimented with it, I had a gay friend, and that was the only time that I ever experienced real confrontation from people, because for so many years, like I said they were basically afraid of me, and when I started hanging out with this person who was known to be gay, I started getting a lot of shit. People trying to beat me up and stuff. Then my mother wouldn't allow me to be friends with him anymore. Cos she's homophobic.

So did you stop?

Yeah, I couldn't hang out with him anymore. It was real devastating because finally I'd found a male friend who I actually hugged and was affectionate to, and we talked about a lot of things. Around that same time, I was putting all the pieces of the puzzle together. He played a big role in that. His name was Meyer Lofton. I haven't spoken to him in years. I heard that he's still in Aberdeen, which is really surprising to me. He hung out with this exchange student, his name was Pachee, and no-one liked him because he was Spanish, and they had a friend who was a lesbian. I can't remember her name, we were friends for a few months until my mother found out that he was gay, and banned him from the house.

You put some provocative gay statements into the lyrics, is that a reflection of that time?

I wouldn't say it was a reflection of that time, I'm just carrying on with my beliefs now. I guess it is [provocative] in a commercial sense, cos of how many albums we've sold, but... in *All Apologies* on this album, one of the lines is, "everyone is gay".

The track that first got me into Nirvana was On a Plain...

We do an acoustic version of that now, and I wish to god we'd recorded it that way, cos it sounds so much better.

What's it about? This is a fan's question!

Classic alienation, I guess. Every time I go through songs, a lot of times I have to change my story, because I'm as much lost as anyone else.

For the most part the way I write is from pieces of poetry, thrown together, you've probably read that somewhere, I've probably repeated it a million times, but that's pretty much how I do it. When I write poetry it's not usually thematic at all, I have plenty of notebooks and when it comes time to write lyrics I just steal from my poems...

Do you put them together very quickly?

Usually, right before I record the vocals! A lot of times the month before we go into the studio, I finish the lyrics. Sometimes the lyrics will come out in about five minutes, but for the most part, ninety percent of it is done at the last minute. There are instances in certain songs, we'd almost have to go through each song, line by line, cos I don't remember... on this album there are more songs that are more thematic, that are actually about something... rather than just pieces of poetry. Like, *Scentless Apprentice* is about the book, *Perfume*, by Patrick Susskind. I don't think I've ever written a song based on a book before.

I really liked that song, Very Ape. I liked the guitar sound...

That was Steve Albini's metal guitar. It's supposedly a really rare guitar, it's all made of aluminum...

Going back to the gay politics and feminist concerns, its very unusual to find bands talking about that, particularly in the format that you're using, which is basically male rock...

Yeah. I think it's getting better though, now that alternative music is finally getting accepted, although it's in a pretty sad form, as far as I'm concerned, but at least the consciousness is there, and that's really healthy for the younger generation.

Have you ever had any problems with that, from the industry or from fans?

Never. Pansy Division covered *Teen Spirit* and reworked the words to *Smells Like Queer Spirit*, and thanked us in the liner notes. I think it said thank you to Nirvana for taking the most pro-gay stance by a commercially successful rock band. That was a real flattering thing... it's just that it's nothing new to any of my friends, because the music we've been listening to for the last fifteen years... I suppose it is different. Do you watch MTV? They are responsible for some of the consciousness recently. I kind of appreciate that. They have these Free Your Mind segments in the news hour, where they report on gay issues and stuff like that. Pretty much in subtle ways they remind everyone how sexist the wave of Heavy Metal was throughout the entire 80s, because all that stuff is completely dead, almost. It's dying fast. I find it really funny to see a lot of those groups like Poison - not even Poison but Warrant and Skid Row, bands like that, desperately clinging to their old identities, but now trying to have an alternative angle in their music, it gives me a small thrill to know that I've helped in a small way to get rid of those people. Or maybe at least to make them think about what they've done in the last ten years.

Nothing has changed really, except for some bands like Soul Asylum who've been around for like twelve years, have been struggling in bars forever, and now they have this opportunity to have their pretty faces on MTV, they still have a better attitude, I think it's healthier. I'd much rather have that than the old stuff. *Did you read much when you were a kid?*

Yeah, just whatever I could get. I went to the library a lot, and I skipped school a lot, especially during high school, junior high, and the only place to go during the day was the library. But I didn't know what to read, it was just whatever I found. During grade school I would read SE Hinton books (note: the most famous is "The Outsider"), I really enjoyed those. I read a lot in class too, when I went to school. Just to stay away from people so I didn't have to talk to them. A lot of times I'd even just pretend to read, to stay away from people... *When did you start to write?*

Probably about fourteen. Junior High. I never took it very seriously. I've never kept personal journals, either. I've never kept a diary, and I've never tried to write stories in the poetry, it's always been abstract. The plan for my life, ever since I can remember was to be a commercial artist. My mother gave me a lot of support in being artistic. She was really complementary of my drawings and paintings. So I was always building up to that. By the time I was in ninth grade I was taking three commercial art classes and I was going to go to art school and my art teacher would enter my paintings and stuff for contests. I wasn't interested in that at all, really. It wasn't what I wanted to do. I knew that I wasn't as good as everyone else thought I was in that town. The ratios aren't that great. I'm a better artist than probably everyone else in that school, but that doesn't say anything if you compare it to a larger city. I knew my limitations. I really enjoy art, I like to paint still... I've always felt the same about writing as well. I know I'm not educated enough to really write something that I would enjoy on the level that I would like to read.

America is so different. When you're feeling bad in England it's like being very slowly submerged, very claustrophobic...

I've felt that way when I've been there. Here it's more like losing your stomach. Like being lost. It's so big, you know. Even though I was growing up in a small town, there was an ocean, and there was a huge city two hundred miles away, there was nothing in between.

You hear that in a lot of American music... in country music. A keening sound, which is totally un-self-conscious. Brits are very self conscious, very mannered.

That would explain why Goth was so much more popular in England... why do people feel embarrassed by that?

Because it was tacky!

It was entertainment! So is anything! So is vaudeville!

Did you ever listen to Joy Division?

I don't think so... I stayed away from Joy Division. I've heard a few of their songs and I know I would really like it, but just the mystique about it and the stories I've heard, I know that's the band to listen to, of all of them. I'm just waiting. But I can't think of anything that I ever listened to, besides Black Sabbath that would ever... I am very claustrophobic, though. Absolutely the worst thought is to be locked in somewhere, in a closet or something...

When did you first visit England?

'89...

Did you enjoy it?

Yeah. The first time especially. But we went through the rest of Europe, and by the seventh week I was ready to die. We were touring with Tad... it was eleven people in a really small Volvo van, with our equipment...

You mean twelve with Tad...

Fifteen...! Depending on whether his stomach was empty or not. He vomited a lot on that tour. But every time I go back to England I like it less and less. It seems so grey and dirty. When I go to New York or LA I don't notice the smog as much as when I go to England. But I've hardly ever been to the countryside in England. I'm sure there are plenty of good places to stay. More and more we stay over at places for a few days after a tour...

When did you first realise that things were starting to break?

I don't know, because we were on tour in Europe. I still don't really know the story. I think probably *Teen Spirit*, because we'd finished thevideo and they started to play it while we were on tour, and I would get reports every once in a while from friends of mine, telling me that I was famous. So it didn't affect me until probably three months after we'd already been famous in America...

Was there one moment when you walked into it and you suddenly realised?

Yeah. When I got home. A friend of mine made a compilation of all the news stories about our band that was played on MTV and the local news programmes and stuff. It was frightening, it just scared me.

How long did it scare you for?

About a year and a half. Up until the last eight months or so. I would say until my child has been born. That's when I finally decided to crawl out of my shell and accept it. I didn't want to go to such ridiculous extremes as U2 has done... I feel like I have an obligation, because I like this band, that I wanted to break it up, I wanted to quit...

Was that in the middle of last year?

That was a time when I wanted to break up the band, but that was because I was having a star fit, and I was starving and because of the Tad tour, but I'm talking about when *Nevermind* got really big... No, that was when the band started to really fail me emotionally, because a lot of it had to do with the fact that we were playing a lot of these outdoor festivals in the daytime. There's nothing more boring than doing that. The audiences are massive and none of them care what band is up on stage. I was just getting over my drug addiction, or trying to battle that, and it was just too much. For the rest of the year I kept going back and forth between wanting to quit and wanting to change our name, cos I still really enjoy playing with

Chris and Dave and I couldn't see us splitting up because of the pressures of success. It's just pathetic, you know? To have to do something like that.

I don't know if there is much of a conscious connection between Chris and Dave and I, when we play live. I don't usually even notice Chris and Dave, I'm in my own world. I'm not saying it doesn't matter whether they're there or not, that I could hire studio musicians or something. I know it wouldn't be the same, but...

For me the original band is you and Chris and Dave...

I consider that the original band too, because it was the first time we had a drummer that was competent. And for some reason, ever since I've been in this band, I've needed a good solid drummer. There are loads of bands that I love that have terrible drummers, but it wasn't right for this music. At least, it isn't right for the music that we've written so far. I'd love to be able to switch places with Dave and try to write some songs that way. There's all kinds of things we could still do.

You haven't really toured for a year...

I've recuperated.

You could have sold more records if you'd kept on touring.

Oh yeah. Kept the record in the charts... I absolutely had to have some time off. The drug addiction didn't get in the way until we had some time off anyhow. I didn't get into the drugs until after the tour. I didn't see the band fall apart because of drugs.

When did the tour stop?

I don't remember... I think February '92.

Why did the drugs happen? Was it just around?

I had done heroin for about a year, off and on. I've had this stomach condition for like five years. There were times, especially during touring where I just felt like a drug addict because I was starving and I couldn't find out what was wrong with me. I tried everything I could think of. Change of diet, pills, everything... exercise, stopped drinking, stopped smoking, and nothing worked. I just decided that if I'm going to feel like a junkie every fucking morning and be vomiting every day then I may as well take a substance that kills that pain. I can't say that that is the main reason why I did it, but it has a lot to do with it. It has a lot more to do with it than most people think.

Did you find out what the stomach thing was?

No.

Do you still get it?

Every once in a while. But for some reason it's just gone away. It's a psychosomatic thing, my mom had it when she was in her early twenties, for a few years, and eventually it went away. She was in a hospital all the time because of it.

Maybe you're feeling a bit better now...

Yeah. Especially since I've been married and have a child, within the last year, my mental state and my physical state have improved almost one hundred percent. I'm really excited about touring again. I haven't felt this optimistic since right before the divorce. You know?

What about the media? Did you find it incredibly disheartening that you'd started this group and you were playing these great songs and suddenly all this weird stuff started happening?

Oh yeah, it affected me to the point of wanting to break up the band all the time.

Was it mainly the Vanity Fair article? (Note: The September 1992 issue of Vanity Fair carried an article about Courtney Love by Lynn Hirschberg, which inter alia raised allegations about Love's drug use during her pregnancy: these resulted in a court hearing in August 1992 about the couple's suitability as parents.)

That started it. There was probably fifty more articles based on that story... I've never paid attention to the mainstream press or media before, so I'd never been aware of people being attacked and crucified on that level. To this day I don't know who Bono's wife is, or if he has a wife, or if he has a girlfriend... I can't help but feel that we've been scapegoated, in a way. I have a lot of animosity towards journalists and the press in general. Because it's happening to me, of course, I'm probably exaggerating it, but I can't think of another example of a current band that's had more negative articles written about them.

Why do you think that is?

A lot of it is just simple sexism. Courtney is my wife, and people could not accept the fact that I'm in love, and that I could be happy. Because she's such a powerful person, and such a threatening person, that every sexist within the industry just joined forces and decided to... just string us up.

From what I can see of Courtney, if you treat her like a threat she'll be one, and if you don't, she won't.

Exactly. That's exactly the way I've always felt.
*When I first met Johnny Rotten, I was very polite to him and very matter of
fact. I think people are very much how you take them. But he can be a real
bastard.*
It's a good defence mechanism...
During punk people were really nasty to each other. Horrible.
I didn't get to see that. By the time that I was into punk, people
were just wallowing in confusion. Should we be sarcastic? Should we
be mean to each other? No-one knew how they were supposed to act
at that point. Almost all my favourite bands are English. It's
amazing how much they've produced...
Do you like that claustrophobic sound?
I think so, yeah. The main reason we recorded with Steve Albini is
he is able to get that sound that sounds like it's in a room that's no
bigger than this. It's not a hall, its not trying to be larger than life.
It's very in your face and real... technically I've learned that the way
to achieve that is to use a lot of microphones. I've known for years,
ever since I started recording, because microphones are so
directional that if you want an ambient sound you need to use a lot
of tracks. Or you need to use an omnidirectional microphone,
farther away from the instruments. So you can pick up the
reverberation from the walls.
How many mikes did you use for this one?
I have no idea, but a lot. We had big old German microphones
taped to the floor and the ceiling and the walls, all over the place.
I've been trying to get producers to do this ever since we've been
recording. I don't know anything about recording but it just seems
so obvious to me that that is what you need to do. I tried to get
Butch Vig to do it, I tried to get Jack Endino to do it, and everyone's
response is, 'that isn't how you record'. Steve Albini proved it to me
on these records, although I don't know exactly how he did it, I just
knew that it had to be that way. He had to have used a bunch of
microphones. It's as simple as that. Which is why live recording
sounds so good, from punk shows. You really get a feel of what was
going on.
Did you re-record a couple of tracks?
No. We remixed a couple, cos the vocals weren't loud enough.
When I brought the tape home of *Heart Shaped Box*, I was singing
this harmony over the melody of *Heart Shaped Box* and I just had to

put it on. Steve is a good recording engineer, but terrible at mixing, as far as I'm concerned. To me, mixing is like doing a crossword puzzle or something. Things that I don't like to do, you know, like math, that's really technical. It drains you, you really have to concentrate on it. Every instrument, there are so many variations in the tones of each instrument, that it can take days to mix a song. If you really want to get anal about it. I'm all for just recording and however it comes out on tape, that's how it should come out. But for some songs it just doesn't work.

There's a really interesting book called The Complete Beatles Recording Sessions (by Mark Lewisohn), which is a record of every studio session they had, and what they did. How they made records. What they did was edit, furiously. A lot of the real classic songs which are about two minutes thirty were chopped really tight. But that was their thing.

It was such a great idea to get some classically trained person like George Martin to produce a pop band.

I really like the slow songs on this album...

They came out really good, and Steve Albini's recording technique really served those songs well. You can really hear the ambience in those songs... it was perfect for that. But for *All Apologies* and *Heart Shaped Box* we needed more... the main complaint was that the vocals weren't loud enough. In every Albini recording I've ever heard, the vocals were too quiet. That's just the way he likes things, and he's a real difficult person to persuade, you know. I mean, he was trying to mix each song within an hour. Which is just not how they work. It was fine for a few songs, but not all of them. You should be able to do what you want and pick the best. I never thought I would enjoy talking about the technical side of recording. I mean, this is as far as it goes. It never made any sense to me before.

I don't think it's a bad thing to talk about. It's just as interesting as talking about sensational press stories... I read through all of the press cuttings and I just thought a lot of this stuff is really boring. It wasn't talking about anything really intelligent a lot of the time, they're just talking about this terrible rock gossip. It's like all the stuff I remember from fifteen years ago.

Fucking hell, haven't we advanced?

I have one criticism: I think you over-reacted on those Victoria Clark letters. I think you gave her publicity... (In October 1992 Cobain and Love left threatening messages on the answerphone of journalist Victoria Clarke, co-author of a proposed unauthorised Nirvana biography).

I know. That's what I tried to tell Courtney... but we weren't in the best of mental states at that time. I totally agree. I mean, that's the first thought that came into my mind, that if we were to address this at all, it was just going to get more press. They dug through our garbage, they lied and fucked their way through so many of my friends, and deceived so many people that I really like in Seattle that I didn't know what to do. It's really hard to be in control of your own press, because my management doesn't know anything about it. How to protect anyone from things like this. Every time we've ever got into a legal battle, we've always ended up just paying people off. We've literally given away money to people like a band called *Nirvana* from Orange County, Los Angeles, fifty thousand dollars, just to stay away from litigation that we easily could have won. I hate that idea because I've always wanted to fight people that are fucking with me unnecessarily. But I don't know how to go about it.
That must be very isolating, cos in that way you are unusual. It's also very punk rock to get a very hostile press.
I'm really not interested in being punk rock anymore!
No, I'm not suggesting you should be, but there is a misapprehension on the part of the media, as well. I know you've joked about this yourself, that you and Courtney have fitted into that mediated Sid & Nancy slot... (The subheadline to the Vanity Fair article read: 'Are Courtney Love...and Kurt Cobain...the grunge John and Yoko? Or the next Sid & Nancy?)
Yeah. Haven't we progressed? You would think that people would want to look into something a bit deeper than something that happened fifteen years ago. And be entertained by a carbon copy of what happened fifteen years ago. It's a boring old story.
Do you feel now that there are contradictions between your ideals and your position? Is that something that worries you?
I don't really know anymore. I think I was probably a lot more contradictory a year and a half ago, because I was blindly fighting and not even knowing what I was fighting for. And to a point I still am. Like I said, I don't really know how to deal with the media. I've had the opportunity of meeting a handful of journalists that I've gotten along with personally and like them as people, and it happens that there's a good chance that they're going to write a good story. A year ago I said absolutely no fucking way will I ever speak in public again. And I'll go out of my way to never show my

face again. I'm not going to let a rock band, or a handful of evil journalists dictate my fucking life.

I was on the road to getting cut up... cutting myself up. But I'm just grateful that I've come across a few people that I trust and I like to talk to. Who happen to be journalists. So that's one thing that I've learned from the last year and a half. I think of some of the people I work with as like my family. Danny Goldberg, who isn't even our manager anymore, who used to own Gold Mountain, he's like my second father. We've been blessed in an enormous way with a handful of people like that, who work at DGC, that doesn't happen with bands at all. It's just a revolving door of people working for you.

In a way you're in a really good position then, because you've got your head around the fact that even if the record doesn't do well - and I think the record will do very well - you've made the record that you wanted to make.

Absolutely. Oh man, I could put out *Flowers of Romance* (Public Image Limited's 'difficult' third album) tomorrow, if that's the record I wanted to make, that's why I'm so excited about this record. I actually want to promote this record, not for the sake of selling records, but I'm more proud of this record than anything I've ever done. We've finally achieved the sound that I've been hearing in my head for ever.

You didn't on Nevermind?

Not at all. It's too slick. I don't listen to records like that at home. I can't listen to that record. I like a lot of the songs. I really like playing some of them live. In a commercial sense I think its a really good record, I have to admit that, but that's in a Cheap Trick way. But for my personal listening pleasure, you know, it's just too slick. I was just pretty much deceived by the studio that we mixed in. I was so burned out at that point... we attempted to mix it ourselves with Butch for a week and a half, and got Andy Wallace in there, and by that point, I wasn't really paying attention. I just didn't really care, as much as I had before.

Were you, or are you a narcoleptic?

No, no... that was just a story I made up... for why I slept so much... I used to find myself sleeping a lot, before shows. A lot of times the backstage area is such a gross scene, I don't want to talk to anybody so I just fall asleep. There's so many people that we know now, so many friends and stuff that I can't ask them to leave. I don't want to act like Axl Rose and have my own bus or my own back room area...

So what happened with the MTV awards? (In September 1992)

Well, apparently Axl was in a really bad mood. Something set him off, probably just minutes before our encounter with him. We were in the food tent and I was holding Frances, and he came strutting by with five of his huge bodyguards and a person with a movie camera. Courtney jokingly screamed out at him, Axl, will you be the godfather of our child? Everyone laughed. We had a few friends around us, and he just stopped dead in his tracks and started screaming at us, all these abusive words. He told me I should shut my bitch up, so I looked over at Courtney and said, shut up, bitch, heh! And everyone started howling with laughter and Axl just kind of blushed and went away. Afterward I'm playing our song, and Dave was screaming, hi Ax!, and Duff wanted to beat Chris up afterwards...

That's the one where Chris hit his head with the guitar. You're all trying to be cool and smash up your instruments, and you really fucked it up, it's really good.

That's happened so many times.

An impressive finale, and you end up looking really stupid, but that's great too.

It was so expected, you know? Should we just walk off the stage, or should we break our equipment again? The emotions that were going through us that whole day, because up until just minutes before we played, we weren't going to play, cos we wanted to play *Rape Me*, and MTV wouldn't let us, and they were just going to replace us if we didn't play *Teen Spirit*, and we ended up playing *Lithium*. I spit on Axl's keyboards when we were sitting on the stage. It was either that or beat him up. We're down on this platform that brought us up hydraulically, you know? And I saw his piano there, and I just had to take this opportunity and spit big goobers all over his keyboards. I hope he didn't get it off in time...

That's great though. That's what should happen in pop, bands bitching at each other. That happens in England all the time.

English people are great at it. Masters at it. God. So entertaining.

Somebody I know met Axl Rose and said he's just this huge closet queen. Anyway. Tell me, were you into Beat Happening? I love that song "Bad Seed"...

Oh yeah, very. It was my introduction to a lot of stuff that preceded that. Like Daniel Johnson and Half Japanese and stuff like that. I'd been into the Velvet Underground for a long time before I heard Beat Happening. I love the Velvet Underground.

I moved to Olympia, from Aberdeen, it was the first place that I moved to, on my own. I was twenty. I'd just started Nirvana and K Records and that whole scene in Olympia turned me on to so much amazing music. The Pastels and the Vaselines and all that stuff. Every couple of years I feel that I've gone as far as I can with being introduced to something new, and then something like that hits me and it gives me life for a few years.

I found that song "Bad Seed" really moving... because it was so hopeless and yet so optimistic - 'a new generation of a teenage nation, this time let's get it right' - yeah, right. Out of this tiny record out of Olympia, yeah, sure. And it kind of happened. It was like a prophecy. Did they knew a lot about English punk?

Yeah, they did. I was turned onto the whole 4AD thing, the Raincoats and the Young Marble Giants (being of course the whole Rough Trade thing...) It was like the first time that I heard punk rock, cos there were all these bands from the last fifteen years, and I'd try to find all these records, and it was a whole scene, these bands that had been going on for like ten years, and it had the same impact on me. It was a completely different world. Young Marble Giants, god. I don't know where I'd be if I hadn't heard that record.

I find it quite odd that you should come from where you come from and love some of this quite mannered English stuff.

It must be the tea my mother fed me all the time...! My mother was really picky and English in that way.

There's a really good interaction that goes on between some Brits and some Americans. I don't know what it is, but it really works. I like American rock because it's unselfconscious. Louie Louie...

Well, I can appreciate that too...

I don't see that in the Raincoats, though, or maybe a little bit in Young Marble Giants...That's a very particular strain, and a very particular period...

...it's so English. I don't talk when we play, but I really enjoy the interaction with Mudhoney, Mark Arm makes these really funny, sarcastic comments to people in the audience. That kind of bond is so great, especially with Mudhoney it's more of a love thing. It isn't violent at all... it translates better in a club, too. That's another reason why I don't give a shit if this record sells. We're guaranteed not to sell half as many records. We know that. That means that we get to go on tour this time and play venues. Three, four thousand seat venues. And we get to stay in the same town for maybe a couple of nights. It's going to be great. It'll be like the first tour that we did with Sonic Youth. Those were some of the best times I've ever had. I think that's a little bit too big, but still... it's a really good environment.

How do you sing? Cos you have a number of voices...

Most of the time I sing right from my stomach. Right from where my stomach pain is... That's where the pain and anger comes from. It's definitely there. Every time I've had an endoscope, they find a red irritation in my stomach. But it's psychosomatic, it's all from anger. And screaming. My body is damaged from music in two ways. Not only has my stomach inflamed from irritation, but I have scoliosis. I had minor scoliosis in junior high, and I've been playing guitar ever since, and the weight of the guitar has made my back grow in this curvature. So when I stand, everything is sideways. It's weird.

You could get that sorted out...

I go to a chiropractor... once in a while. You can't really correct scoliosis, because it's a growth in the spine... your spine grows through your adolescent years in a curvature. Most people have a small curvature in their spine anyhow, mine's just... some people have it really bad and have to have metal braces... so it gives me a back pain all the time. I was in pain all the time too. That really adds to the pain in our music. It really does. I'm kind of grateful for it.

Tell me, I have to ask what happened with the gun thing. Was that all bullshit? (The most recent published scandal about the couple at that time concerned an incident on June 4 1993 when Courtney Love called the police on Cobain at their Seattle home during a domestic dispute. The police confiscated a selection of guns and ammunition)

Oh yeah. Total bullshit. That's another thing that has made me want to just give up. A couple of weeks ago... I never choked my wife... and every report, even in Rolling Stone... in the police report for some reason... I've seen a copy of the police report, and Courtney was wearing a choker, you know what those are? I ripped in off of her, and it turned out in the police report that I choked her. We weren't even fighting. We weren't even arguing, we were playing music too loud and the neighbours complained, called the police on us. It was the first time that they've ever complained, and we've been practising in the house for a long time...

Very Axl Rose!

That's it, you see. Old shit. That's the way they expect you to behave, because you're a controversial rock star. The police were really nice about it, though. To tell you the truth, I couldn't believe it. See, there's this new law, passed that month in Seattle, where when there's a domestic violence call, they have to take one or the other to jail. So Courtney and I, the only argument we got into was who was going to go to jail for a few hours. And they asked us, out of the blue, are there any guns in the house, and I said no. Because I didn't want them to know there were guns in the house. I have an M-16 and two hand guns. They're put away, there are no bullets in them, they're up in the closet, and they took them away. I can get them back now. I haven't bothered to get them back yet, but it was all just a ridiculous little situation. It was nothing. And it's been blown up out of proportion. It's just like I feel like people don't believe me. Like I'm a pathological liar. I'm constantly defending myself. People still haven't evolved enough to question anything that's printed. I'm really bad at that too. I still believe a lot of things that I read.

But you must behave badly sometimes?

Sure. Courtney and I fight. We argue a lot. But I've never choked my wife. It's an awful fucking thing to be printed, to be thought about you. You know. We haven't had any problems, any bad reports, any negative articles written about us in a long time. We thought we were finally over it. Our curse had worn itself out.

It must also be because people have perceived you as a threat.

I think Courtney is more of a threat than I am.

But I bet your success is a threat to some people...

It was a threat to the metal bands...

So what are the plans for the album? Tour it a little bit?

Tour for about six weeks, in the states, starting October. Then I don't want to commit to anything until we see how I feel physically after that. Maybe we'll go to Europe. I'm sure we'll be over in Europe to support this record within a year, but I'm not sure when. I don't want to set a whole year's worth of touring up...

There seems to be a tension, in that you defined yourself at a time as being influenced by punk, and part of punk was that it wasn't cool to be successful. Did you feel that, and has it caused you problems?

That's not how I perceived early punk. I thought that the Sex Pistols wanted to rule the world. And I was rooting for them. But then American punk rock in the mid 80s became totally stagnated and elitist. It was a big turn-off for me. I didn't like it at all. But at the same time, I had been thinking that way for so long, that it was really hard for me to come to terms with success. But I don't care about it now. There's nothing I can do about it. I'm not going to put out a shitty record on purpose to make sure... that would be ridiculous. But I would probably have done that a year and a half ago. I would have gone out of my way to make sure that the album was even noisier than it is, but we did this record the way we wanted to. *I'm glad about that. It worried me a bit that you might get into that trap. Cos it's not interesting.*

That defeats the whole reason of making music. I've been validated beyond anything. When we could sell out the Vogue in Seattle, which holds about three hundred people... I would gladly go back to that. I'll gladly go back to playing in front of twenty people - if I'm still enjoying it. That's one of the most positive things about this new record. I know we're not going to have the fringe millions who don't enjoy music, who aren't into our band for any other reason than as a tool to fuck.
What have been the worst temptations of being successful?

Nothing I can think of, except Lollopalooza. They offered us a guarantee of like six million dollars, and that's way more money than... we're going to break even on this tour because we're playing theatres, and the production is so expensive at this level. But other than that, I've never thought of the Guns and Roses, Metallica and U2 offers as any kind of offer. It was just never a reality to me. Or Chris and Dave. So... those were the only temptations that I can think of that someone would actually consider a temptation.
Were you quite misanthropic for a long time?

Oh yeah. Absolutely. I hated everybody. I always managed to have at least one close friend at a time, through most of my life. There have been years where I would just put up with my best friend, and not really like the person. But since I've been in the band and since I've known Chris and I have a handful of friends that are great, but... I had a typical, narcissistic attitude until a year and a half ago before Courtney became pregnant. 'How dare you bring a child into this life?'you know? That kind of attitude is really selfish. There's no way I can think that now. I have no right to say something like that.

TRANSCRIPT: Marc Issue Robinson

to hell with

RICHARD MILWARD

BECS AND MARIE HAVE DIRTY MOUTHS

If Scott smashed that window, they were going to smash him. Ever since Beechwood Infants he went around trying to scare the pants off Becs and Marie, but after a bit it didn't totally faze them. Becs licked a scratch on her arm, standing in her torn-effect jeans while Marie made another vodka-Tango. They were meant to be going to the cinema with Scott and they wanted to get out before the curfew kicked in, but all he wanted to do was throw rocks at them and put his face against the glass like a serial killer. He was annoying. The winter dark was the spookiest part, and as Becs and Marie stood all jazzed up it made them feel cold. It was dead easy getting into an 18 with a bit of face on, but if Scott didn't grow up they'd miss it anyway - they were playing loads of Halloweeny films at the UGC that night, maybe that's why Scott was acting so sinister.

"He's a fuckin complete tosser," Marie said, tucking her hands under her smooth armpits. Becs nodded then just shrugged, trying to neck some of that drink but the orange was going all over. Becs' mam and step-dad were out doing the quiz or doing each other, and Becs wanted to be gone before they got back to all the mess.

Marie put her face up to the kitchen window, flat hands either side, but there wasn't much to look at except for moving beech trees and that dark. She couldn't see Scott outside and soon the glass got really cloudy from her breath, so she took her eyes off and looked at Becs. Ideas were charging round her like a headache, although it could've been the vodkas.

"Have you still got that fuckin thingy… that Polaroid camera?" she asked, just as Becs finished off the Tango.

"You what?"

Marie was the sort of girl who never went down without a fight. In reality Scott was just as scared of ghosts and things as them - he was really sensitive about the history textbooks at school, for example. The Collins one was the worst, with photos of black Americans getting lynched and a Chinese guy with his head lopped off, and just the thought of it made Marie shiver and laugh. She had this idea of dressing herself as one of those victim people, posing in front of the window, and scaring the hell out of Scott - it'd probably be a load of hassle, but it looked like they wouldn't make the cinema now and they had to get their kicks somehow. Becs sniffled then ran upstairs, smiling her head in half. It was hard to find the right stuff, but Marie sprinkled a bit of flour on her cheeks and soon she looked quite dramatic. Zombies were easy. It reminded her of their phase listening to loads of Nic Endo and Atari Teenage Riot - her and Becs didn't exactly go round all vamped up and dracula-like, but the people on the CD covers had pretty white faces. Except for Carl Crack of course, because he was coloured. Anyhow, Becs came back in the kitchen with the Kodak camera, and nearly weed herself laughing - Marie was that scary.

For Marie, maturity came with shagging a tall lad on the swings at Pallister Park when she was twelve, but it felt ever so childish looking round the kitchen for things to hang yourself with. Marie's mam's advice was to wait for your first period before you start thinking about sex - at least then your body says you're ready, but Marie didn't know if the willy or the egg made her bleed that night. It was pretty weird. Scott was actually quite good-looking, but neither Becs or Marie had laid him before - once they did tie him to his bed and strip off his clothes though. It was hilarious feeling like s+m mistresses, sexy versions of teachers at school - that was probably in their industrial phase as well. Scott blushed like mad, but his knob was okay for a fourteen year-old and he was quite fit with his swimmer's body and all that. But now everything seemed so boring in Middlesbrough, what with the curfew and the school exams and boys being idiots. It was the perfect lifestyle going round and bedding a load of them, but after a while you realise they're all immature little kids. Marie licked her fingers and smudged up her mascara - it was amazing how dead the Revlon made her look.

"This film isn't fuckin cheap, you know," Becs said, charging up the flash. She smiled at Marie though, then helped slap on a bit more flour and they went round looking for a noose but all they could find was her dad's blue fishing-wire. It looked pretty authentic round Marie's neck, though. Becs put on 'Live at Brixton Academy 1999' then got a stool from the front room, coming back and standing Marie on top of it. The screwy white noise was blaring out, and it put the girls really in the mood to torture Scott - after all he'd ruined their evening. Sniggering, Becs tightened Marie to the solid light fitting, which got kind of dim with Marie's head in the way. She was frightening - Becs was dead quaky as Marie stood on tippy-toes, but they both found it hilarious.

"Don't strangle me then you daft bitch," Marie giggled, as Becs took all the slack out of the fish-wire. You could tell it was cutting into Marie's neck, but it looked dead genuine and she tried not to move about too much. They were sick little freaks.

"Suck your fuckin cheeks in, and shove your eyes back," Becs went, doing the impression for her. Becs glanced outside the kitchen for shapes or movement, while her mate hung out like one of those history photos but there was no sign of Scott. They knew he'd be back though, since the curfew made the streets so dull and the last thing he'd want would be to get escorted home. Becs sighed then struck the Polaroid light at Marie, blue-tacking the horrid squares behind the curtains for Halloween boy as they developed. She made sure not to include the chintzy stool, so Marie looked like she was in mid-air and totally screwed. Imagine if they were so frightened of Scott they decided to lynch themselves; it was quite a stupid idea really.

"By the way," said Becs, with her eyes in the lens, "don't fall off that fuckin stool, or you are gonna kill yourself."

Even though it was spooky, Marie grinned and it made her spine twinkle, but she felt pretty retarded at the same time.

Becs fired more autopsy from the black plastic, curling her pink lips while the film unloaded. She liked the way the pics zapped into life as you flapped them, showing a silly suicide. On the steamy windows she made a chessboard, and all the pieces were killed girls. Becs was starting to wish they'd saved the Polaroid for their hols or their mates at school, but as it was they were having a good time. On some of the photos you could even see Marie smirking, but she always had to have the last laugh really. Marie was probably too good-looking for a corpse - she looked good in heroin chic, and she looked good in fishing tackle. Becs laughed, but then she felt bad because the night was well and truly wrecked - the UGC was only open til about eleven, and it'd take at least til midnight to get the flour off Marie and get her looking right again. She glanced at her watch, and it didn't even seem like Scott was about any more - they could always post him the photos.

Just then, the front door went bang and Becs lost her concentration, slipping slightly on the messy floor. She took the camera from her face and went to check the noise out, all jiggly as she stomped out of the kitchen. It was freezing in the hall and she shuddered in her heels, then shit herself as a brick or something came crashing off the porch window. Then Scott's head banged right up against the glass. Becs jumped and the camera flew out across the lino, and Marie jumped and the chintzy stool flew out from under her.

MICHAEL SMITH

LUCY LOCKETT

So I found myself going round to a glass penthouse in a converted chocolate factory overlooking one of the old Saatchi galleries... I lived in a council house box room that was roughly twice the size of my bed, a box room that backed on to a leaky noisy railway bridge where the troll could quite easily have dossed about waiting to eat the little billy goats... maybe she was hungry for a bit of rough and I was hungry for a bit of glamour, and she certainly seemed to offer that...

She cut quite a dash with those swinging sixties good looks, Victorian petticoats and $500 white Manolo Blahniks, which she was fond of stamping emphatically like a flamenco dancer in a tantrum when I wouldn't let her have her own way... it was her most stylish move, and had me completely suckered... why is it beautiful women are always such a pain in the arse? The temper and the foot stamping thing drove me crazy... it was obvious to me that for all my sins I was going to have to train her up and break that brat in her as mercilessly and despotically as possible, so we fought and shouted like spoiled siblings for much of the time, neither of us backing down, just getting worse and worse until she'd generally try to attack me and claw my eyes out, and then I'd catch her claws and bend her arms behind her back a little more roughly than I had to, and then she'd try to bite me, so I'd end up having to pin her down on the floor by her arms and hair while she went red with rage and started crying... and all it ever did was bring us closer together...

The opposites attract thing was kind of the driving dynamic with us two; I loved her old school English poshness, a quality I'd pretty much despised in people before, in that stupid Northern way, a chip on our collective shoulders the size of a closed down coal mine... but she just carried herself in a certain way and pulled it all off with such glamour and sparkle... she was the archetypal English Rose, the flower of Thames Valley finishing schools, and could carry off words like *Crikey!* and *Huzzar!* with effortless elegance and panache, all in the loveliest rich chocolatey posh Windsor voice ... it fixed in my mind an idea of the nobility and romance of the English way that has swelled my heart with ridiculous pride ever since...

Growing up in the husk of a North Eastern ghost town a generation after the last ship had been built, the place that inspired the Blade Runner sets, there was never much pride or romance when it came to my ideas of England... I grew up at the end of the train line, next to the rugged and desolate North Sea, a sea of winds and storms and Vikings, of vast empty scrubby sand dunes and nuclear power stations... my childhood memories of the sea are of diving into the choppy waves off the Elephant Rock and coming out in horrible rashes because of all the sewage, or coming across seals washed up on shore with no heads and stumpy necks like raw hamburgers...

She remembers the big water very differently, the river was her roots and it ran through all her early memories... she remembered waterside inns, royal cygnets and swans, Wogan and Parkey and old army majors fishing away exquisitely lazy afternoons on the banks of the Thames on a lovely posh stretch of river near the Queen's gaff at Windsor... I remember her happiest when she'd fondly name all the river birds on our summer strolls through the London parks: the coots, the crested greebs, the moorhens and the mallards...

She grew up spending weekends on a narrow boat called Lucy Lockett; her dad had bought it to celebrate her birth, and many of her most treasured memories took place on this boat, in locks, in country canals, on holidays, on leisurely Sunday afternoons... her dad sold it just before we met, and whenever she mentioned it a real regret and sadness hit her, because Lucy Lockett represented her childhood, and selling it represented its loss... this sadness was so weighty and so stubbornly deep rooted it was part of her, it had helped to shape her and just couldn't be put right... lots of things went wrong in her life and something inside her just couldn't get past them and hankered back to a fantasy of idyllic childhood she set up like a shrine in her memories... and as a consequence one of the keynotes of her personality was she just couldn't bear to let anything go... her house was full of junk that needed to be binned, bags and bags of it piled up next to cupboards... the bedroom was left in such disarray it resembled a nest... cupboards' worth of clothes on every inch of floor space, coat hangers waiting to spike your feet, an assault course every time you tried to climb into bed...

Lucy was a photographer, and I wonder if that also sprang from her need to fix and capture transient moments forever, to embalm the past… that's what worries me when I think about her rattling around that gingerbread house all on her lonesome, coming to terms with the fact she's on her own again; that and the fact she needs people round her a lot more than I do… I've never particularly needed other people that much- except, that is, when I've fallen in love with them; then, and when they've gone…

SUBSCRIPTIONS

To Hell with Publishing
44 Ossington Street
London W2 4LY
Fax: 020 7243 1415
Email: info@tohellwithpublishing.com
Website: www.tohellwithpublishing.com

Single issue: £16 (inc. p&p)
International single issue: £20 (Air) £17 (Sea)

Cheques payable to: To Hell with Publishing Ltd
Or buy online at www.tohellwithpublishing.com
3 issues per annum

Co-ordinator: Dean Ricketts, The Watch-Men Agency
Legal Representation: Jonathan Dembo, All Our Business
Design: Murray & Sorrell FUEL